Computer Acronym Handbook

DONALD D. SPENCER

Prentice-Hall, Inc.
Englewood Cliffs, N.J.

Prentice-Hall International, Inc., *London*
Prentice-Hall of Australia, Pty. Ltd., *Sydney*
Prentice-Hall of Canada, Ltd., *Toronto*
Prentice-Hall of India Private Ltd., *New Delhi*
Prentice-Hall of Japan, Inc., *Tokyo*

Library of Congress Cataloging in Publication Data

Spencer, Donald D
Computer acronym handbook.

1. Electronic data processing--Acronyms.
I. Title.
QA76.S676 001.6'4'0148 73-20221
ISBN 0-13-164863-2

Printed in the United States of America

To my brother Bob

A Word from the Author

The technological advances during the past twenty years have been so widespread that there has been a steadily increasing use of computers by noncomputer personnel. Many areas that were reasonably familiar only to those trained in computer science and data processing ten years ago are today part of the curriculum of many universities and colleges. This is, of course, a proper trend, but the rate of transfer from computer groups to new organizations appears to have accelerated enormously in recent years.

Associated with this widespread technology has been the creation of many new computers and a computer vocabulary. Since many computer words and phrases tend to be rather long and clumsy to remember, this shortcut vocabulary handbook consisting of acronyms, abbreviations, symbols and nicknames, was created. This handbook facilitates communication between personnel working in the computer field as well as for specialists in other fields—management in government, business, and industry; teachers and administrators in education—and between laymen.

The primary purpose of this book is to provide the readers of computer literature with a handbook for rapidly deciphering the many acronyms and abbreviations that are being used in this literature. This book should not be considered as a standard and in no way seeks to authorize the listed acronym or abbreviation as the only approved one for the word or phrase.

I believe that this collection of computer acronyms and abbreviations will be useful to college students, teachers, systems analysts, journalists, professional programmers, engineers, mathematicians, librarians, EDP managers, and anyone else who has occasion to read computer literature.

The acronym has been adopted wholesale by the computer field. In fact, the acronym vocabulary is now so large that it makes one wonder if much communicative value might not be lost. Even within the computer field the extensive use of acronyms and abbreviations can cause real difficulties in communication between those with different specialities: engineers, programmers, systems analysts, teachers, and managers. These difficulties may be greatly magnified when one outside the computer field tries to read computer literature.

Many terms, such as EDP, IBM, and CRT are commonly used, even by laymen. There are, however, many terms that are used only by personnel directly associated with the computer field. How important is knowing the definition of an acronym? It is as important as the time lost searching for it or the consequences of not being able to find it. The newcomer who has just been introduced to computer language is usually amazed and confused at the number of acronyms and abbreviations that he must use: ANSI, FORTRAN, CAI, COBOL, EOJ, CDC, ENIAC, ACM. The understanding of these terms is taken for granted by people already working in the computer field.

ARRANGEMENT

The terms in this book are arranged in strict alphabetical and numerical order. The ampersands (&), hyphen (-), and virgule (/) are ignored in the arrangement. For example, EDPM follows EDP, C&A follows CA, IPL-V follows IPL, D/A follows DA, and A2 follows A.

DEFINITION

Each acronym or abbreviation is followed by one definition. If a term has more than one meaning, the meaning is listed on an additional line. Supplementary information is enclosed within parentheses to help clarify the meaning.

HOW TO USE AN ACRONYM

The correct way to use an acronym in a technical article, report, or book is to explain it to your reader the first time it appears. For example, if you are writing about a Critical Path Technique, it would be preferable to begin by using the term Critical Path Technique (CPT) fully spelled out and then use the abbreviation CPT throughout the rest of your publication. The use of acronyms allows one to save space and to avoid endless repetition. If the author is sure that the acronym is known to all the readers, he may omit the previous definition step. A case would be where the acronym was one of common usage such as FORTRAN, IBM, BASIC, ADP, or DPMA, and the readers were people working in the computer field.

NOTE TO READERS

This book is as up to date and complete as possible. The information was collected over a five-year period. However, new terms and computer names are constantly being added to the computer language. These will be collected by the author for possible inclusion in subsequent editions of this book.

Donald D. Spencer

ACKNOWLEDGMENTS

I would like to thank the computer manufacturers, computer consulting firms, universities and colleges, and computer publishing houses whose extensive and intensive publications in the computer science area have contributed so much in making this work possible. I also wish to thank my wife, Rae, who prepared the manuscript for publication.

A

A	Accumulator
A	Address
A0	Automatic Coding System
A1	Automatic Coding System
A2	Automatic Coding System
AA	Arithmetic Average
AAA	American Accounting Association
AAAS	American Association for the Advancement of Science
AABP	Aptitude Assessment Battery-Programming
AACE	American Association of Cost Engineers
AACSCEDR	Associate and Advisory Committee to the Special Committee on Electronic Data Retrieval
AAL	Absolute Assembly Language
AAPL	Additional Programming Language (Western Electric)
AAS	Arithmetic Assignment Statement
AAS	Automated Accounting System
AAVD	Automatic Alternate Voice/Data
ABA	American Bankers Association
ABA	American Bar Association
ABAC-II	A Basic Coursewriter, Version II
ABACUS	Air Battle Analysis Center Utility System

ABACUS	Fast FORTRAN Compiler
ABBR	Abbreviate
ABBR	Abbreviation
ABC	Automatic Bandwidth Control
ABC	Automatic Coding System
ABL	Atlas Basic Language
ABM	Automated Batch Mixing
ABRACE	Brazilian Association of Electronic Computers
ABV	Absolute Value
AC	Accumulator
AC	Airborne Computer
AC	Alternating Current
AC	Analog Computer
AC	Automatic Checkout
AC	Automatic Computer
ACA	American Communications Association
ACA	Automatic Communications Association
ACAP	Automatic Circuit Analysis Program
ACBS	Accrediting Commission for Business Schools
ACC	Accumulator
ACCAP	Autocoder to COBOL Conversion Aid Program (IBM)
ACCESS	Aircraft Communication Electronic Signaling System

ACCESS	Automatic Computer Controlled Electronic Scanning System
ACCT	Account
ACCUM	Accumulate
ACCUR	Accuracy
ACCUR	Accurate
ACE	Acceptance Checkout Equipment
ACE	Algebraic System
ACE	Animated Computer Education
ACE	Automatic Checkout Equipment
ACE	Automatic Computer Evaluation
ACE	Automatic Computing Engine
ACF	Area Computing Facilities
ACFG	Automatic Continuous Function Generation
ACID	Automatic Classification and Interpretation of Data
ACIS	Association for Computing and Information Sciences
ACK	Acknowledge
ACL	Applications Control Language
ACL	Association for Computational Linguistics
ACL	Atlas Commercial Language
ACLS	American Council of Learned Societies
ACM	Association for Computing Machinery
ACMAC	ACM Accreditation Committee

ACME	Advanced Computer for Medical Research
ACME	Association of Consulting Management Engineers
ACM-GAMM	Association for Computing Machinery/German Association for Applied Mathematics and Mechanics
ACMS	Army Command Management System
ACMSC	ACM Standards Committee
ACNA	Auerbach Computer Notebook for Accountants
ACOM	Automatic Coding System
ACOPP	Abbreviated COBOL Preprocessor
ACP	Advanced Computational Processor (Sylvania)
ACP	Aerospace Computer Program
ACPA	Association of Computer Programmers and Analysts
ACR	Accumulator Regulator
ACRE	Automatic Checkout and Readiness Equipment
ACS	Advanced Computer Services (HIS)
ACS	Advanced Computer System (IBM)
ACS	American Chemical Society
ACS	Armament Control System
ACS	Assembly Control System (IBM)
ACS	Australian Computer Society
ACS	Automated Communications Set
ACS	Automatic Checkout System

ACS	Auxiliary Core Storage
ACSS	Analog Computer Subsystem
ACT	Actual
ACT	Algebraic Compiler and Translator
ACT	Automatic Code Translation
ACTRAN	Audocoder-to-COBOL Translating Service
ACTS	Automatic Computer Telex Services
ACU	Arithmetic and Control Unit
ACU	Automatic Calling Unit
ACUTE	Accountants Computer Users Technical Exchange
AD	Advanced Design
A-D	Analog to Digital
A/D	Analog to Digital
ADA	Automatic Data Acquisition
ADAC	Automatic Direct Analog Computer
ADACC	Automatic Data Acquisition and Computer Complex
ADAM	Absolutely Devine Automatic Machine (NBS)
ADAM	A Data Management System
ADAM	Advanced Data Management System
ADAM	Associometrics Data Management System
ADAPS	Automatic Display and Plotting System
ADAPSO	Association of Data Processing Service Organizations

ADAPT	Air Material Command Developed APT
ADAPT	Data Processing Compiler
ADAS	Automatic Data Acquisition System
ADAT	Automatic Data Accumulator and Transfer
ADC	Air Data Computer
ADC	Airborne Digital Computer
ADC	Analog-to-Digital Converter
ADC	Automatic Data Collection
ADCON	Analog-to-Digital Converter
ADD	Addition
ADD	Address
ADD	Aerospace Digital Development (UNIVAC)
ADDAR	Automatic Digital Data Acquisition and Recording
ADDAS	Automatic Digital Data Assembly System
ADDR	Address
ADE	Automated Design Engineering
ADEC	Aiken Dahlgren Electronic Calculator
ADEPO	Automatic Dynamic Evaluation by Programmed Organizations
ADES	Automatic Digital Encoding System
ADI	American Documentation Institute
ADIC	Analog-to-Digital Conversion
ADIDAC	Argonne National Laboratory Computer

ADINET	Administrative Network Service
ADIOS	Automatic Digital Input-Output System
ADIS	Association for Development of Instructional Systems
ADIS	Automatic Data Interchange System
ADIT	Analog-Digital Integration Translator
ADL	Automatic Data Link
ADMA	Automatic Drafting Machine
ADMIN	Administration
ADMIRAL	Automatic and Dynamic Monitor with Immediate Relocation, Allocation and Loading
ADMIRE	Automated Diagnostic Maintenance Information Retrieval System
ADONIS	Automatic Digital On-Line Instrumentation System
ADP	Airborne Data Processor
ADP	Automatic Data Processing
ADPC	Automatic Data Processing Center
ADPCM	Association for Data Processing and Computer Management
ADPE	Automatic Data Processing Equipment
ADPE	Auxiliary Data Processing Equipment
ADPP	Automatic Data Processing Program
ADPS	Automatic Data Processing System
ADPSO	Association of Data Processing Service Organizations

ADR	Address
ADR	Address Register
ADRAC	Automatic Digital Recording and Control
ADRS	Address
ADRT	Analog Data Recorder Transcriber
ADS	Accurately Defined System
ADS	Advance Data Systems
ADSC	Automatic Data Service Center
ADS-TP	Administrative Data Systems Teleprocessing System
ADSUP	Automated Data Systems Uniform Practices
ADT	Advanced Design Team
ADT	Automatic Data Translator
ADU	Automatic Dialing Unit
ADX	Automatic Data Exchange
AE	Application Engineer
AE	Arithmetic Element
AE	Arithmetic Expression
AEC	Atomic Energy Commission
AECT	Association for Educational Communications & Technology
AED	ALGOL Extended for Design
AED	Automated Engineering Design
AEDP	Association for Educational Data Processing
AEDS	Association for Educational Data Systems

AEGIS	An Existing General Information System
AEI	Associated Electrical Industries Ltd. (Great Britain computer manufacturer)
AERA	American Educational Research Association
AERIS	General Purpose Computer
AESOP	An Evolutionary System for On-Line Processing
AF	Air Force
AF	Audio Frequency
AFAC	Automatic Coding System
AFC	Automatic Frequency Control
AFCAL	Association Française de Calcul (French Computing Association)
AFCALTI	French Associations of Computing and Information Processing
AFCC	Air Force Command and Control
AFCEA	Armed Forces Communications and Electronics Association
AFDDA	Air Force Director of Data Automation
AFG	Analog Function Generator
AFIP	American Federation of Information Processing
AFIPS	American Federation of Information Processing Societies
AFL	Abstract Family of Languages
AFL	Animated Film Language

AFM	Automatic Flight Management
AFNOR	French Standards Association
AFOSR	Air Force Office of Scientific Research
AFRA	French Association of Automatic Control
AGC	Automatic Gain Control
AGDIC	Astro Guidance Digital Computer
AGE	Aerospace Ground-support Equipment
AGILE	Autonetics General Information Learning Equipment
AGSP	Atlas General Survey Program
AI	Automatic Input
AI	Automation Institute
AIA	Aerospace Industries Association
AIAA	American Institute of Aeronautics and Astronautics
AIB	American Institute of Banking
AICA	Automatico Associazione Italiana per Il Calcolo (Italian Computer Assocation)
AICA	International Association for Analog Computing
AICE	American Institute of Consulting Engineers
AICHE	American Institute of Chemical Engineers
AICPA	American Institute of Certified Public Accountants

AID	Airline Interline Development (UNIVAC)
AID	Algebraic Interpretive Dialogue
AIDE	Automated Integrated Design Engineering
AIDS	Administrative Information Data System
AIDS	Automatic Integrated Debugging System
AIEE	American Institute of Electrical Engineers
AIIE	American Institute of Industrial Engineers
AIM	Air Isolated Monolithic
AIM	American Institute of Management
AIMACO	Air Material Command version of FLOWMATIC
AIME	American Institute of Mechanical Engineers
AIME	American Institute of Mining, Metallurgical, and Petroleum Engineers
AIMES	Automated Inventory Management Evaluation System
AIMS	Automated Industrial Management System
AIMS	Automated Information and Management Systems
AIP	American Institute of Physics
AIPE	American Institute of Plant Engineers

AIRCON	Automated Information and Reservations Computer Oriented Network
AIRS	Automatic Information Retrieval System
AISC	Association of Independent Software Companies
AIST	Automatic Informational Station
AIT	American Institute of Technology
AJAC	*Australian Journal of Applied Science*
AL	Assembly Language
ALA	American Library Association
A-LANGUAGE	Auxiliary Language
ALAS	Asynchronour Look Ahead Simulator
ALC	Programming Language
ALCAPP	Automatic List Classification and Profile Production
ALCOM	Algebraic Compiler
ALCOR	ALGOL Converter
ALD	Analog Line Driver
ALERT	Automated Linguistic Extraction and Retrieval Technique
ALERT	Military Computer (Honeywell)
ALERT	Programming Language similar to APL
ALFTRAN	ALGOL To FORTRAN Translator
ALG	Algebraic
ALGEC	Soviet Algorithmic Language for Economic Problems

ALGO	Algebraic Compiler
ALGO	Algorithm
ALGOL	Algorithmic Language
ALGOL 58	1958 version of the Algorithmic Language
ALGOL 60	1960 version of the Algorithmic Language
ALGOL 68	1968 version of the Algorithmic Language
ALGUM	Programming Language
ALI	Automated Logic Implementation
ALICS	Assembly Language
ALIS	Advanced Life Information System
ALLOC	Allocate
ALMO	Algorithmic Machine Oriented Language (Russian meta-compiler)
ALMS	Analytic Language Manipulation System
ALP	Assembly Language Program
ALP	Associated Learning Project
ALP	Autocode List-processing Language
ALP	Automated Learning Process
ALPAK	Programming Language
ALPHA	Alphabetic
ALPHA	Automatic Programming System (U.S.S.R. M-20 computer)
ALPS	Advanced Linear Programming System (HIS)
ALPS	Associated Logic Parallel System

ALPS	Automated Library Processing Service
ALREN	Applied Logic Report Generator
ALT	Alternate
ALTAC	Algebraic Transistorized Automatic Computer Translator
ALTRAN	Algebraic Translator (extension to FORTRAN)
ALTRAN	Assembly Language Translator (Xerox Corp.)
ALU	Arithmetic and Logical Unit
ALWAC	Alex-Wenner-Gren Automatic Computer
ALWAC USERS	ALWAC Users Organization
AM	Amplitude Modulation
AM	Auxiliary Memory
A/M	Auto/Manual
AMA	American Management Association
AMA	American Manufacturers' Association
AMA	American Marketing Association
AMA	American Medical Association
AMA	Automatic Memory Allocation
AMACUS	Automated Microfilm Aperture Card Updating System
AMBIT	Algebraic Manipulation by Identity Translation
AMC	Association of Management Consultants
AMC	Automatic Message Counting
AMECOPI	Mexican Association for Computing and Information Processing

AMFIS	American Microfilm Information Society
AMIT	Ampex to IBM Tape
AMJM	*American Journal of Mathematics*
AML	Animated Movie Language
AML	Applied Mathematics Laboratory (David Taylor Model Basin)
AMOS	Associative Memory Organization System (syntax-directed compiler language)
AMOS	Automatic Meteorological Observation Station
AMP	Ampere
AMP	Associative Memory Processor
AMPS	Automatic Message Processing System
AMR	Atlantic Missile Range
AMR	Automated Management Reports
AMR	Automatic Message Registering
AMS	Administrative Management Society
AMS	American Mathematical Society
AMTCL	Association for Machine Translation and Computational Linguistics
AMTRAN	Automatic Mathematical Translation
AN	Alphanumeric
ANACOM	Analog Computer
ANATRAN	Analog Translator
ANCP	Automatic Coding System
AND	Logical Operator
A-NEW	A New Project

ANL	Argone National Laboratory
ANS	American Nuclear Society
ANSI	American National Standards Institute
ANZAAS	Australian and New Zealand Association for the Advancement of Science
AOC	Automatic Output Control
AOCS	Alpha Omega Computer System
AOL	Application Oriented Language
AOS	Add or Subtract
AOSP	Automatic Operating and Scheduling Program
AP	Application Program
AP	Applications Processor
AP	Argument Programming
AP	Associative Processor
AP2	Rice Institute version of ALGOL
APA	American Psychological Association
APADS	Automatic Programmer and Data System
APAR	Automatic Programming and Recording
APAREL	A Parse-Request Language
APB	Automatic Programming Language (HIS/Bull GAMMA Computer)
APC	Automatic Phase Control
APCHE	Automatic Programming Checkout Equipment
APE II	Arizona Pedagogical II computer

APEHC	All-Purpose Electronic Computer
APERC	All-Purpose Electronic Computer
APEXC	All-Purpose Electronic Computer
APICS	American Production and Inventory Control Society
APIN	Association for Programmed Instruction in the Netherlands
APL	A Programming Language
APL	Associative Programming Language
APL/360	A Programming Language on the IBM System/360 computer
APNIC	Automatic Programming National Information Centre (Brighton Technical College, England)
APOLLO	General Purpose Computer (Raytheon)
APP	Associative Parallel Processor
APP	Auxiliary Power Plant
APPECS	Adaptive Pattern Perceiving Electronic Computer System
APPROX	Approximate
APS	Auxiliary Program Storage
APS	Auxiliary Publications Service (ASIC)
APT	Augmented Programming Training
APT	Automatic Picture Transmission
APT	Automatic Programmed Tools
APT	Automation Planning and Technology
APT III	Extended version of APT
APTS	Automatic Picture Transmission System

APX III	Automatic Programming System Extended
AQ	Any Quantity
AQL	Acceptable Quality Level
ARC	Argonne Reactor Computation System
ARC	Automatic Relay Calculator
ARC	Average Response Computer
ARCCOS	Inverse cosine
ARCCOT	Inverse cotangent
ARCCSC	Inverse cosecant
ARCSEC	Inverse secant
ARCSIN	Inverse sine
ARCTAN	Inverse tangent
ARE	Advanced Real-time Executive
ARE	Automated Responsive Environment
AREA	Association of Records, Executives and Administrators
A REG	A Register
ARG	Argument
ARGUS	Automatic Routine Generating and Updating System
ARGUS	Process Control Computer (mfg. by Ferranti, Ltd.)
ARIEL	Programming Language
ARITH	Arithmetic
ARITH-MATIC	Automatic Coding System
ARL	Association of Research Libraries

ARM	Automated Route Management (IBM)
ARMA	American Records Management Association
ARPA	Advanced Research Projects Agency (Office of the Secretary of Defense)
ARQ	Automatic Error Correction
ARQ	Automatic Request for Repetition
ART	Automatic Coding System (UNIVAC)
ART	Automatic Reporting Telephone
ARTIC	Associometrics Remote Terminal Inquiry Control System
ARTOC	Army Tactical Operations Center
ARTS	Advanced Radar Tracking Control System (UNIVAC)
ARTS	Automated Radar Terminal System
ARU	Audio Response Unit
ASA	American Standards Association (now ANSI)
ASA	American Statistical Association
ASAE	American Society of Agricultural Engineers
ASAP	As Soon As Possible
ASAS	Computer-Assisted Student Affairs System
ASBO	Association of School Business Officials
ASC	Advanced Scientific Computer
ASC	American Society for Cybernetics
ASC	Associative Structure Computer
ASC	Atlantic Systems Conference

ASCII	American Standard Code for Information Interchange
ASC 15	Advance System Controller Model 15
ASCATS	Apollo Simulation Checkout and Training System
ASCC	Automatic Sequence Controlled Calculator (also called MARK 1)
ASCE	American Society of Civil Engineers
ASCENT	Assembly System, Central Processor (CDC 6000 Series)
ASE	Automatic Support Equipment
ASEE	American Society for Engineering Education
ASGN	Assign
ASI	American Standards Institute
ASIS	American Society for Information Science (Formerly ADI)
ASIST	Advanced Scientific Instruments Symbolic Translator
ASIST	Macro Level Assembler
ASK	Automatic Service Komputer
ASL	Association for Symbolic Logic
ASLIB	Association of Special Libraries and Information Bureau
ASLT	Advanced Solid Logic Technology
ASM	Association for Systems Management
ASME	American Society of Mechanical Engineers
ASNE	American Society of Naval Engineers

ASOP	Automatic Scheduling and Operating Program
ASP	Association Storing Processor
ASP	Associative Structures Package
ASP	Attached Support Processor (IBM)
ASP	Automatic Schedule Procedures
ASPA	American Society for Public Administration
ASPEP	Association of Scientists and Professional Engineering Personnel
ASPER	Assembly System Peripheral Processors (CDC 6000 Series)
ASQC	American Society for Quality Control
ASR	Accumulators Shift Right
ASR	Automatic Send-Receive
ASSE	American Society of Safety Engineers
ASTD	American Society for Training and Development
ASTIA	Armed Services Technical Information Agency
ASTM	American Society for Testing Materials
ASTME	American Society of Tool and Manufacturing Engineers
ASTRAL	Analog Schematic Translator to Algebraic Language
ASV	Automatic Self-Verification
ASVIP	American Standard Vocabulary for Information Processing

AT	Automatic Ticketing
AT3	Compiler Language (Later called Math-Matic)
ATA	Air Transport Association
ATA	Associate in Technical Arts
ATAR	Automated Travel Agents Reservation
ATC	Air Traffic Control
ATC	Automation Training Center
ATDS	Airborne Tactical Data System
ATE	Automatic Test Equipment
ATLAS	Automatic Test Language for Avionics Systems
ATLAS	Digital Computer (mfg. by Ferranti Ltd.)
ATOLL	Acceptance, Test Or Launch Language
ATP	Automated Test Plan
ATS	Administrative Terminal System (IBM)
AT&T	American Telephone and Telegraph Co.
AU	Arithmetic Unit
AUDREY	Audio Reply
AUG	Argument
AUIS	Analog Input-Output Unit
AUNT	Automatic Universal Translator
AUTO	Automatic
AUTOCODE	Autocoding scheme on several computers manufactured in Great Britain

AUTOCODER	Programming Language
AUTODIN	Automatic Digital Network (Dept. of Defense)
AUTODOC	Automated Documentation
AUTOMAP	Automatic Machining Program (IBM)
AUTOMATH	FORTRAN-like programming system (Honeywell)
AUTOMN	Automation
AUTONET	Automatic Network Display
AUTONOTE	Information Storage and Retrieval System
AUTOPIC	Automatic Personal Identification Code (IBM)
AUTOPROMT	Automatic Programming of Machine Tools (IBM)
AUTOPSY	Automatic Operating System
AUTOSEVOCOM	Automatic Secure Voice Communications
AUTOSPOT	Automatic System for Positioning Tools
AUTOSTATE	Automated Data Systems Analysis Technique
AUTOSTATIS	Automatic Statewide Theft Inquiry System
AUTOTIMER	Automatic Timing and Machine Evaluation Routine
AUTOVON	Automatic Voice Network
AUTRAN	Automatic Utility Translator
AUTSIM	Automatic Simplification (FORMAC)
AUX	Auxiliary

AV	Audio Visual
AVAIL	Availability
AVC	Automatic Volume Control
AVR	Automatic Volume Recognition
AWCS	Air Weapons Control System
AXD	Auxiliary Drum
AXLE	Axiomatic Programming Language

B

B	Base
B	Binary
B	Bit
B	Blank
B	Block
B	Burroughs Corp.
B15	Automatic Coding System
BA	Binary Add
BAAS	British Association for the Advancement of Science
BACAIC	Boeing Airplane Company Algebraic Interpretive Computing System
BACE	Basic Automatic Checkout Equipment
BACE	British Association of Consulting Engineers
BADGE	Base Air Defense Ground Environment
BAL	Basic Assembly Language
BALGOL	Burroughs Algebraic Compiler
BALITAC	Automatic Coding System
BALLOTS	Bibliographic Automation of Large Library Operations using Time Sharing
BAM	Basic Access Method
BAMS	Bulletin of the American Mathematical Society

BANK LN PROC	Bank Loan Processor (ITT)
BANKPAC	Banking Application Program
BAP	Basic Assembly Program
BAR	Base Address Register
BASEBALL	Automatic Question-Answerer
BASIC	Automated Information System
BASIC	Basic Algebraic Symbolic Interpretive Compiler
BASIC	Basic Automatic Stored Instruction Computer
BASIC	Battle Area Surveillance and Integrated Communications
BASIC	Beginner's All-purpose Symbolic Instruction Code
BASICPAC	Basic Processor and Computer
BASIS	Bank Automated Service Information System
BASIS	Burroughs Applied Statistical Inquiry System
BASYS	Basic System
BBL	Basic Business Language
BC	Binary Code
BC	Binary Counter
BC	Burroughs Corp.
BCAC	British Conference on Automation and Computation
BCCL	Birkbeck College Computation Laboratory
BCD	Binary Coded Decimal
BCDIC	Binary Coded Decimal Interchange Code

BCH	Binary Coded Hollerith
BCI	Binary Coded Information
BCIP	Belgium Centre for Information Processing
BCL	Burroughs Common Language
BCL	Programming Language (Atlas Computer)
BCM	Basic Control Monitor (Xerox Sigma Series)
BCO	Binary Coded Octal
BCOM	Burroughs Computer Output-to-Microfilm
BCPL	Bootstrap Combined Programming Language
BCS	Biomedical Computing Society
BCS	British Computer Society
BCU	Binary Counting Unit
BCW	Buffer Control Word
BD	Binary Decoder
BD	Binary Divide
B-D	Binary-to-Decimal
BDAM	Basic Direct Access Method
BDC	Binary Code
BDC	Binary Decimal Counter
BDD	Binary to Decimal Decoder
BDIC	Binary Coded Decimal Interchange Code
BDP	Business Data Processing
BDT	Binary Deck to Binary Tape
BDU	Basic Display Unit

BEA	Business Education Association
BEAC	Boeing Engineering Analog Computer
BEAM	Burroughs Electronic Accounting Machine
BEAME	British Electrical and Allied Manufacturers
BEE	Business Efficiency Exhibition
BEEF	Business and Engineering Enriched FORTRAN
BEFAP	Bell Laboratories FORTRAN Assembly Program
BEL	Bell Character
BEL	Bharat Electronics, Ltd. (computer manufacturer in India)
BELL	A Floating-Decimal Interpretive System
BELL MACRO-FAP	Bell Laboratories Macro FORTRAN Assembly Program
BEMA	Business Equipment Manufacturers Association
BER	Bit Error Rate
BER	Buffer
BESK	Swedish Digital Computer
BESM	Digital Computer (U.S.S.R.)
BESS	Binary Electromagnetic Signature
BEST	Business EDP Systems Technique (NCR)
BEST	Business Electronic Systems Technique
BEST	Business Equipment Software Techniques

BEX	Broadband Exchange
BF	Base File
BFPDDA	Binary Floating Point Digital Differential Analyzer
BFR	Buffer
B-H	Binary-to-Hexadecimal
BICS	Burroughs Inventory Control System
BIDEC	Binary to Decimal Converter
BIE	British Institute of Engineers
BIEE	British Institute of Electrical Engineers
BIL	Block Input Length
BIMAC	Bistable Magnetic Core
BIN	Binary
BINAC	Binary Automatic Computer
BIO	Biological Information-processing Organization
BIOMED	Biomedical Support Package (UNIVAC 1108)
BIONICS	Biology and Electronics
BIOR	Business Input-Output Rerun Compiling System
BIPCO	Built-In-Place Components
BIRE	British Institute of Radio Engineers
BIRS	Basic Indexing and Retrieval System
BIS	Business Information System
BISAM	Basic Indexed Sequential Access Method (IBM)
BIT	Binary Digit

BIT	*Nordisk Tidsskrift for Informationsbehandling* (computer journal published by SIP)
BITS	Binary Digits
BIX	Binary Information Exchange
BIZMAC	Business Machine Computer (RCA)
BJF	Batch Job Foreground
BJM	Between Job Monitor
BKS	Autocontrol System (Philco 2000)
BKSP	Backspace
BL	Bell Telephone Laboratories
BLADE	Basic Level Automation of Data Through Electronics
BLADES	Bell Laboratories Automatic Design System
BLESSED	Bell Little Electrodata Symbolic System for the Electrodata
B-LINE	Bell Line Drawing Language
BLIS	Bell Laboratories Interpretive System
BLK	Block
BLM	Basic Language Machine
BLNK	Blank
BLNSYS	Operating System with Braille Capabilities
BLODI	Block Diagram Compiler
BLODIB	Block Diagrammed Compiler (Bell Labs)
BLT	BASIC Language Translator
BM	Binary Multiply

BMD	Biomedical Computer Programs (Univ. of Calif.)
BMEWS	Ballistic Missile Early Warning System
BMI	Battelle Memorial Institute
BMS	Business Management System (CSC)
BN	Binary Number
BNCS	British Numerical Control Society
BNF	Backus Normal Form
BNS	Binary Number System
B-O	Binary-to-Octal
BOB	Bureau of the Budget
BOCOL	Basic Operating Consumer Oriented Language
BOEING COMPILER	Boeing Programming System
BOLD	Bibliographic On-Line Display
BOM	Basic Operating Monitor (IBM 1800)
BOP	Binary Output Program
BOS	Background Operating System
BOS	Basic Operating System
BOSS	Boeing Operational Supervisory System
BOSS	Business Oriented Software System (PDP-8 series)
BOSS	Operating System
BOT	Beginning of Tape
BPAM	Basic Partitioned Access Method (IBM)

BPI	Bits Per Inch
BPI	Bytes Per Inch
BPKT	Basic Programmer Knowledge Test
BPM	Batch Processing Monitor (Xerox Sigma Series)
BPS	Basic Programming System
BPS	Bits Per Second
BPS	Bytes Per Second
BQL	Basic Query Language
BR	Branch
BR	Bunker Ramo Corporation computer designation
BRAINIAC	Build-it-yourself computer kit
BRIDGE	Engineering Subsystem of ICES
BRL	Ballistic Research Laboratories
BRLESC	Ballistic Research Laboratories Electronic Scientific Computer
BRT	Binary Run Tape
BRUIN	Brown University Interpreter
BS	Backspace character
BS	Binary Subtract
B/S	Bits per Second
B.S.	British Standard
BSAM	Basic Sequential Access Method (IBM)
BSB	Backspace Block
BSC	Binary Synchronous Communications
BSCA	Binary Synchronous Communications Adapter

BSCN	Bit Scan
BSDC	British Standard Data Code
BSF	Backspace File
BSI	British Standards Institute
BSR	Blip-Scan Ratio
BTAM	Basic Tele-processing Access Method (IBM)
BTD	Binary to Decimal
BTDL	Basic Transient Diode Logic
BTL	Beginning Tape Label
BTL	Bell Telephone Laboratories
BTSS	Basic Time Sharing System
BUF	Buffer
BUGS	Brown University Graphics System
BUGSYS	Programming Language (for preparing animated movies)
BUGTRAN	FORTRAN Debugging Aid
BUIC	Back-Up Interceptor Control
BUILD	Base for Uniform Language Definition
BUR	Bureau
BW	Bandwidth
BYP	Bypass character

C

C	Cell
C	Character
C	Clear
C	Computer
C	Control
C	Cycles per Second
C 10	Programming Language (similar to COLINGO)
CA	Computers and Automation
C & A	Computers and Automation
CAA	Computer Assisted Accounting
CABAL	Compiler-compiler language
CACDP	California Association of County Data Processors
CACM	Communications of the Association for Computing Machinery
CAD	Computer Access Device
CAD	Computer-Aided Design
CAD	Computer-Aided Detection
CAD	*Computer Applications Digest*
CAD	Computer Assisted Design
CADAM	Computer-Graphics Augmented Design and Manufacturing System
CADAR	Computer Aided Design, Analysis and Reliability

CADC	Cambridge Automatic Digital Computer
CADEP	Computer Aided Design of Electronic Products
CADET	Computer-Aided Design Experimental Translator (M.I.T.)
CADETRAN	FORTRAN-like compiler (West Point)
CADETS	Classroom Aided Dynamic Educational Time-Sharing System
CADIC	Computer-Aided Design of Integrated Circuits
CADSS	Combined Analog-Digital Systems Simulator
CAE	Compagnie Europeene d'Automatisme Electronique (French computer manufacturer)
CAE	Computer Aided Education
CAE	Computer Assisted Enrollment (IBM)
CAFE	Computer Aided Film Editor (language)
CAGE	Computerized Aerospace Ground Equipment
CAI	Computer Administered Instruction
CAI	Computer Aided Instruction
CAI	Computer Analog Input
CAI	Computer Assisted Instruction
CAI	Computer Automation, Inc.
CAI/OP	Computer Analog Input/Output
CAL	Computer Animation Language

CAL	Computer Assisted Learning
CAL	Conversational Algebraic Language (version of JOSS)
CAL	Cornell Aeronautical Laboratory
CAL	Course Author Language
CALC	Calculate
CALC	Conversational Interpretive Program
CALCOMP	California Computer Products, Inc.
CALINT	Interpretive System
CALM	Computer Assisted Library Mechanization
CAM	Central Address Memory
CAM	Computer Address Matrix
CAM	Computer-Aided Manufacturing
CAM	Content Addressable Memory
CAMA	Centralized Automatic Message Accounting
CAMP	Compiler for Automatic Machine Programming
CAMP	Computer Applications of Military Problems User's Group
CAMP	Computer Assisted Mathematics Program
CAMP	Computer Assisted Movie Production
CAMP	Controls and Monitoring Processor
CAMPUS	Comprehensive Analytical Model for Planning in the University Sphere
CAN	Cancel Character
CANS	Computer-Assisted Network Scheduling System

CANUNET	Canadian University Computer Network
CAOS	Completely Automatic Operational System
CAP	Capacitor
CAP	Card Assembly Program
CAP	Classroom Assembly Program (M.I.T.)
CAP	Compool Assembler Program
CAP	Computer Analysts and Programmers of England
CAP	Computer Assisted Production
CAP	Control Assembly Program
CAP	Council to Advance Programming
CAPAC	Capacity
CAPAL	Computer and Photographic Assisted Learning (Eastman Kodak Co.)
CAPE	Communications Automatic Processing Equipment
CAPM	Computer Aided Patient Management
CAPS	Computer Assisted Problem Solving
CAPT	Conversational Parts Programming Language
CAR	Channel Address Register
CAR	Computer Assisted Research
CARBINE	Computer Automated Real-time Betting Information Network
CARD	Compact Automatic Retrieval Display
CARDCODER	Card Automatic Code System (IBM)
CARR	Carrier

CARS	Computer Aided Routing System
CARS	Computerized Automotive Reporting Service
CART	Central Automated Replenishment Technique
CART	Central Automatic Reliability Tester (Texas Instruments)
CART	Computerized Automatic Rating Technique
CASD	Computer Aided System Design
CASDAC	Computer-Aided Ship Design and Construction
CASE	Computer Aided System Evaluation
CASE	Computer Automated Support Equipment (HIS)
CASE	Concept Attainment Simulation Experiment
CASES	Computerized Applicant Search, Evaluation and Selection
CASE SOAP III	Modified version of Soap II
CASSA	Continental Army Command Automated System Support Agency
CAST	Clearinghouse Announcements in Science and Technology
CAT	Compile and Test
CAT	Computer Aided Teaching
CAT	Computer Aided Translation (CDC 3600)
CAT	Computer-Assisted Testing
CATLG	Catalog

CATO	Compiler for Automatic Teaching Operation (a FORTRAN-like language)
CATPROC	Catalog Procedure
CATS	Computer-Aided Teaching System
CAUML	Computers and Automations Universal Mailing List
CAUSE	College and University System Exchange
CAW	Channel Address Word
CAX	Community Automatic Exchange
CBI	Compound Batch Identification
CBI	Computer-Based Instruction
CBIS	Computer-Based Instructional System
CBMA	Canadian Business Manufacturers Association
CBMS	Conference Board of the Mathematical Sciences
CC	Card Column
CC	Carriage Control
CC	Central Computer
CC	Central Control
CC	Computer Community
CC	Condition Code
CC	Cross Correlation
C & C	Command and Control
CCAP	Communications Control Application Program
CCB	Change Control Board

CCC	Canadian Computer Conference
CCC	Computer Communication Console
CCD	Committee on Computing and Disadvantaged (ACM)
CCD	Computer Controlled Display
CCIA	Console Computer Interface Adapter
CCIS	Command Control Information System
CCITT	Comité Consultatif Internationale Pour Telegraphie et Telephonie
CCL	Control Language
CCM	Communications Controller-Multichannel
CCR	Computer Characteristics Review (Keydata Corp.)
CCROS	Card Capacitor Read-Only Storage
CCS	Computer Consulting Service
CCS	Conversational Compiling System (Xerox)
CCSA	Common Carrier Special Applications
CCVS	COBOL Compiler Validation System
CCW	Channel Command Word
CD	Card
CD	*Computer Design* (periodical)
CDA	Command and Data Acquisition
CDA	Control Data Australia Pty., Ltd.
CDC	Call Directing Code
CDC	Code Directing Character
CDC	Configuration Data Control

CDC	Control Data Corporation
CDCE	Central Data-Conversion Equipment
CDE	Certificate in Data Education
CDE	Certified Data Educator (SDE)
CDG	Coding
CDI	Control Data Institute
CDJM	*Canadian Journal of Mathematics*
CDL	Common Display Logic
CDL	Computer Description Language
CDL	Computer Design Language (ALGOL-like language)
CDP	Central Data Processor
CDP	Centralized Data Processing
CDP	Certificate in Data Processing (DPMA)
CDP	Checkout Data Processor
CDP	Communication Data Processor
CDPC	Central Data Processing Computer
CDPC	Commercial Data Processing Centers
CDR	Computer Display Review (Keydata Corp.)
CDR	Critical Design Review
CDRL	Contractor Data Requirements List
CDS	Computer Duplex System
CDSE	Computer Driven Simulation Environment
CDT	Control Data Terminal
CDU	Central Display Unit

CDW	Computer Data Word
CE	Civil Engineering
CE	Compagnie Europeene d'Automatisme Electronique (French computer firm)
CE	Computer Engineer
CE	Computer Engineering Ltd. (Great Britain computer manufacturer)
CEDPA	California Educational Data Processing Association
CEI	Computer Extended Instruction
CEI	Contract End Item
CEIS	California Education Information System
CEMON	Customer Engineering Monitor (IBM)
CENG	Control Engineering
CENSOR	Central Processor (manufactured by Standard Radio & Telefon, Sweden)
CEP	Civil Engineering Package
CEP	Computer Entry Punch
CEPA	Civil Engineering Program Applications (IBM User's Group)
CERI	Centre for Educational Research and Innovation
CERN	European Organization for Nuclear Research
CETA	Automatic Translation Research Center (France)
CETIS	European Center for the Processing of Scientific Information

CF	Central File
CF	Context Free
CF	Control Footing
CF	Conversion Factor
CF	Count Forward
CFL	Context-Free Language
CFM	Cathode Follower Mixer
CFSTI	Clearinghouse for Federal Scientific and Technical Information
CGA	Contract Go Ahead
CG-1	Course Generator
CH	Character
CH	Control Heading
CHAMP	Character Manipulation Procedures
CHAN	Channel
CHAR	Character
CHE	Channel End
CHEMPOS	Chemical Engineering Language
CHI	Computer Human Interaction
CHILD	Cognitive Hybrid Intelligent Learning Device
CHK	Checkpoint
CHR	Character
CI	Card Input
CI	Cost Improvement
CIA	Central Intelligence Agency
CIA	Communications Interrupt Analysis

CIA	Computer Industry Association
CIA	Computer Interface Adapter
CIB	COBOL Information Bulletin
CID	Centre for Information and Documentation
CIDAS	Conversational Interactive Digital/Analog Simulator (IBM)
CIF	Central Index File
CII	Compagnie Internationale pour l'Informatique (French electronic company)
CIM	Computer Input Multiplexer
CIMCO	Card Image Correction
CIO	Central Input-Output Multiplexer
CIOCS	Communication Input and Output Control System
CIOU	Custom Input/Output Unit
CIPM	Council for International Progress in Management
CIPS	Canadian Information Processing Society
CIR	Circuit
CIRCLE	Digital Computer (Hogan Laboratories)
CIRRUS	Digital Computer (Australia)
CISCO	Compass Integrated System Compiler
CIT	Compagnie Industrielle de Telecommunication (French computer manufacturer)
CITAB	Computer Instruction and Training Assistance for the Blind

CITAC	Process Control Computer (Mfg. by the French firm CIT)
CIU	Community Information Utility
CIU	Computer Interface Unit
CJ	*Computer Journal* (British periodical)
CK	Check
CKT	Circuit
CL	Computational Linguistics
CL	Control Language
CL	Conversion Loss
CL-1	Programming System
CLA	Clear and Add
CLA	Communication Line Adapter
CLAS	Computer Library Applications Service
CLASP	Computer Language for Aeronautics and Space Programming (NASA)
CLASS	Computer-based Laboratory for Automation of School Systems
CLASSMATE	Computer Language to Aid and Simulate Scientific, Mathematical, and Technical Education
CLC	Course Line Computer
CLDAS	Clinical Laboratory Data Acquisition System
CLEAN	Commonwealth Law Enforcement Assistancc Network
CLEP	College-Level Examination Program
CLIP	Compiler Language for Information Processing

CLK	Clock
CLMS	Clinical Laboratory Management System
CLP	Cornell List Processor (Cornell University)
CLR	Clear
CLR	Computer Language Recorder
CLR	Computer Language Research
CLS	Clear and Subtract
CLS	Close
CLS	COBOL Language Subcommittee
CLS	Common Language System
CLS	Concept Learning System
CLT	Communication Line Terminal
CLT	Computer Language Translator
CLU	Central Logic Unit
CLU	Circuit Lineup
CM	Card Management System (CDC)
C/M	Cards per Minute
CM	Centimeter
CM	Central Memory
C/M	Communications Multiplexer
CM	*Computer Management* (British publication)
CM	Core Memory
CMC	COBOL Maintenance Committee
CMC	Communications Mode Control
CMD	Command

CMD	Core Memory Driver
CMI	Computer Managed Instruction
CML	Current Mode Logic
CMP	Computational
CMP	Computer
CMPL	Complement
CMPLX	Complex
CMPTR	Computer
CMS	Compiler Monitor System
CMT	Conversational Mode Terminal (Friden)
CNCT	Connect
CND	Condition
CNL	Circuit Net Loss
CNR	Italian National Research Council
CNSL	Console
CNT	Count
CNT	Counter
CNTRL	Central
CO.	Company
COAM	Customer Owned And Maintained
COAMS	Customer Owned And Maintained System
COAX	Coaxial
COAX	COBOL Preprocessor
COBESTCO	Computer Based Estimating Technique for Contractors
COBIS	Computer Based Instruction System

COBLIB	COBOL Library
COBLOC	Codap Language-Block Oriented Compiler
COBOL	Common Business Oriented Language
COC	Coded Optical Character
CODAP	Control Data Assembly Program
CODAS	Customer-Oriented Data Retrieval and Display System
CODASYL	Conference on Data Systems Languages
CODATA	Committee on Data for Science and Technology (established by ICSU)
CODEL	Computer Developments Limited Automatic Coding System
CODES	Computer Design and Evaluation System
CODIC	Color Difference Computer
CODIC	Computer Directed Communications
CODIL	Control Diagram Language
CODIT	Computer Direct to Telegraph
COED	Computer Operated Electronic Display
COEF	Coefficient
COF	Computer Operations Facility
COFIL	Core File
COG	Computer Operations Group
COGENT	Compiler Generator and Translator
COGO	Coordinate Geometry
COIN	Complete Operating Information

COINS	Computer and Information Sciences
COINS	International Symposia on Computer and Information Science
COL	Column
COL	Computer Oriented Language
COLASL	Compiler—Los Alamos Scientific Laboratory
COLIDAR	Coherent Light Detection and Ranging
COLINGO	Compile On-Line and Go
COLT	Communication Line Terminator
COLT	Computerized On-Line Testing
COLT	Control Language Translator
COLT 22	Computer Oriented Language Translator
COM	Computer-Output-Microfilm
COMA	Computer Operations Management Association
COMAC	Continuous Multiple Access Collator
COMAR	Computer, Aerial Reconnaissance
COMET	Computer Operated Management Evaluation Technique
COMIT	Compiler, Massachusetts Institute of Technology (string handling and pattern-matching language)
COMLOGNET	Combat Logistics Network
COMLOGNET	Communications Logistics Network
COMM	Communication
COMMEN	Compiler Oriented for Multi-

	programming and Multi-processing Environments
COMMEND	Computer-Aided Mechanical Engineering Design System
COMMERCIAL TRANSLATOR	Automatic Coding System
COMMON	Small IBM Computer Users Group
COMP	Compilation
COMP	Computer
COMPAC	Computer Program for Automatic Control
COMPACT	Compatible Algebraic Compiler and Translator
COMPACT	Computer Planning and Control Technique (HIS)
COMPASS	Comprehensive Assembly System (CDC 3000 Series)
COMPEL	Compute Parallel
COMPIL	Compilation
COMPLEAT	Compleat Programmer
COMPOOL	Communications Pool (Xerox)
COMPREHENSIVE	Automatic Coding System (Whirlwind I - M.I.T.)
COMPRESS	Computer Research, Systems and Software
COMPROG	Computer Program
COMPSO	Computer Software and Peripheral Show
COMPULTEST	CAI Problem-Oriented Programming Language
COMRADE	Computer-Aided Design Environment

COMSL	Communication System Simulation Language
COMTRAN	Commercial Translator (IBM)
CON	Constant
COND	Condenser
COND	Condition
CONF	Conference
CONS	Consultant(s)
CONSORT	Conversational System with On-line Remote Terminals
CONSUL	Control Subroutine Language
CONTRAN	Control Translator (HIS)
CONTRANS	Conceptual Thought, Random-Net Simulation
CONST	Constant
CONT	Continue
CONT	Control
CONV	Convert
CONV	Converter
COOL	Checkout Oriented Language
COOL	Control Oriented Language
COOP	Automatic Coding System
CO-OP	CDC Users Association
COORD	Coordinate
COP	Computer Optimization Package
COP	Customer Order Processing
COPAC	Continuous Operation Production Allocation and Control

COPE	Communications Oriented Processing Equipment
COPE	Console Operator Proficiency Examination
COPI	Computer-Oriented Programmed Instruction
CORAL	Class Oriented Ring Association Language (M.I.T.)
CORAL	Computer On-Line Real-time Applications Language
CORBIE	Programming System
CORC	Cornell Programming Language (Cornell University)
CORDIC	Coordinate Rotation Digital Computer
CORE	Computer Oriented Reporting Efficiency
CORP.	Corporation
CORREGATE	Correctable Gate
COS	Compatible Operating System
COS	Concurrent Operating System (UNIVAC)
COS	Cosine
COSATI	Committee on Scientific and Technical Information
COSBA	Computer Services Bureau Association (Great Britain)
COSEC	Cosecant
COSECH	Hyperbolic Cosecant
COSH	Hyperbolic Cosine
COSMIC	Computer Software Management and Information Center

COSMOS	Computer Oriented System for Management Order Synthesis (IBM)
COSOS	Conference on Self-Operating Systems
COSPUP	Committee on Science and Public Policy (National Academy of Sciences)
COSRIMS	Committee on Support of Research in Mathematical Sciences
COT	Cotangent
COTRAN	COBOL to COBOL Translator (converts IBM second generation source language COBOL statements to IBM System/360 COBOL)
COURSEWRITER	Text-processing Language
CP	Card Punch
CP	Central Processor
CP	Clock Pulse
CP	Communication Processor
CP	Control Panel
CP	Control Processor
CP	Customized Processor (IBM System/4 Pi)
CPC	Card Programmed Calculator (IBM)
CPC	Clock-Pulse Control
CPC	Computer Process Control
CPC	Computer Program Component
CPC	Computer Programming Concepts
CPC	Cycle Program Control
CPC	Cycle Program Counter
CPCEI	Computer Program Contract End Item
CPD	Cards Per Day

CPD	Consolidated Programming Document
CPDS	Computer Program Design Specification
CPE	Central Processing Element
CPE	Central Programmer and Evaluator
CPFF	Cost Plus—Fixed Fee
CPI	Characters Per Inch
CPI	Computer Prescribed Instruction
CPIF	Cost Plus—Incentive Fee
CPIP	Computer Program Implementation Process
CPL	Combined Programming Language
CPL	Computer Program Library
CPM	Cards Per Minute
CPM	Critical Path Method
CPM	Cycles Per Minute
CPP	Card Punching Printer
CPP	Computer Professionals for Peace
CPPS	Critical Path Planning and Scheduling
CPRG	Computer Personnel Research Group
CPS	Central Processor System
CPS	Characters Per Second
CPS	Conversational Programming System
CPS	Critical Path Scheduling
CPS	Cycles Per Second
CPSS	Common Programming Support System (Xerox)

CPT	Critical Path Technique
CPTA	Computer Programming and Testing Activity
CPU	Central Processing Unit
CR	Card Reader
CR	Carriage Return
CR	Cathode Ray
CR	Command Register
CR	Computing Reviews (ACM)
CRAFT	Computerized Relative Allocation of Facilities Technique (IBM)
CRAM	Card Random Access Memory (NCR)
CRC	Collins Radio Co.
CRD	Capacitor-Resistor-Diode Network
CRDSC	Current Research and Development in Scientific Documentation
CRIS	Command Retrieval System (Litton)
CRJE	Conversational Remote Job Entry
CRO	Cathode Ray Oscilloscope
CRT	Cathode Ray Tube
CRT	Charactron Tube
CRTOG	Cartography
CRTU	Combined Receiving and Transmitting Unit
CS	Card Station
CS	Centisecond; one hundredth of a second
CS	Channel Status

C/S	Characters per Second
CS	Check Sorter
CS	Coding Specification
CS	Commercial Standard
CS	Computer Science
CS	Customer Service
C/S	Cycles per Second
CS-1	Compiling System-One (UNIVAC)
C & S	Computers and Systems
CSA	Canadian Standards Association
CSA	Computer Sciences Association
CSA	Computer System Analyst
CSA	Computer Systems Association
CSC	Civil Service Commission
CSC	Computer Sciences Corp.
CSC	Computer Society of Canada
CSC	Cosecant
CSCH	Hyperbolic Cosecant
CSD	Computer Science Department
CSD	Computer Science Division
CSD	Computer System Director
CSD	Constant-Speed Drives
CSE	Control Systems Engineering
CSE	Core Storage Element
CSEC	Centisecond; one hundredth of a second
CSIRAC	Commonwealth Scientific & Industrial Research Automatic Computer

CSIRO	Commonwealth Scientific and Industrial Research Organization
CSL	Code Selection Language
CSL	Computer Sensitive Language
CSL	Control and Simulation Language
CSM	Continuous Sheet Memory
CSMA	Communications Systems Management Association
CSMP	Continuous System Modeling Program (IBM)
CSP	Commercial Subroutine Package (IBM)
CSSA	Computer Society of South Africa, Ltd.
CSSL	Continuous System Simulation Language
CSSR	Comprehensive System of Service Routines (M.I.T.)
CSST	Computer System Science Training
CST	Computer Science Theater
CT	Commercial Translator
CT	Computer Technology
CT	Count
CT	Counter
CTC	Conditional Transfer of Control
CTC	Contact
CTDS	Code Translation Data System
CTL	CAGE Test Language
CTL	Checkout Test Language
CTL	Control

CTL	Core Transistor Logic
CTMC	Communication Terminal Module Controller (UNIVAC)
CTP	Command Translator and Programmer
CTR	Center
CTR	Counter
CTRL	Control
CTS	Communications Terminal Synchronous
CTS	Conversational Terminal System
CTS	Conversational Time-Sharing
CTSS	Compatible Time-Sharing System (M.I.T.)
CTU	Central Terminal Unit
CU	Control Unit
CUAS	Computer Utilization Accounting
CUBE	Cooperating Users of Burroughs Equipment
CUBOL	Computer Usage Business Oriented Language
CUE	Computer Updating Equipment
CUE	Configuration Utilization Efficiency
CUE	Cooperating Users Exchange
CUES	Computer Utility Educational System
CULP	Computer Usage List Processor
CUP	Communications User Program
CUR	Current

CURES	Computer Utilization Reporting System
CUSIP	Committee on Uniform Security Identification Procedures
CUT	Control Unit Tester (UNIVAC)
CUTS	Computer Utilized Turning System
CVIC	Conditional Variable Incremental Computer
CW	Clockwise
CW	Compiled With
CW	*Computerworld* (weekly periodical)
CWBS	Contract Work Breakdown Structure
CX	Central Exchange
CXA	Programming Language (CDC 3600)
CY	Calendar Year
CY	Cycle
CYCLONE	Digital Computer (Iowa State University)

D

D	Deci
D	Decimal
D	Deleted
D	Digit
D	Digital
D	Diode
D	Display
D	Double Precision Constant (FORTRAN)
D	Double Word
DA	Decimal Add
DA	Decimal to Analog
DA	Define Area
DA	Design Automation
DA	Differential Analyzer
DA	Digital to Analog
D-A	Digital to Analog
DA	Discrete Address
DAB	Display Assignment Bits
DAB	Display Attention Bits
DAC	Design Augmented by Computers (General Motors)
DAC	Digital-to-Analog Converter
DAC	Display Analysis Console

DACC	Direct Access Communications Channel
DACE	Data Acquisition and Control Executive (Hewlett-Packard)
DACOM	Datascope Computer Output Microfilmer (Eastman Kodak)
DACON	Digital to Analog Converter
DACS	Data Acquisition Control System (IBM 1800)
DAFT	Digital-Analog Function Table
DAIR	Driver Aid, Information and Routing
DAISY	Double Precision Automatic Interpretive System
DAM	Data Association Message
DAM	Descriptor Attribute Matrix
DAM	Direct Access Memory
DAM	Direct Access Method
DAMIT	Data Analysis Computer Program by M.I.T.
DAMPS	Data Acquisition Multiprogramming System (IBM System/360)
DAMSEL	ADAM Sensitive Language
DAP	Digital Assembly Program (EAI)
DAPAL	Daystrom Powerplant Automation Language
DAPS	Direct Access Programming System (GE)
DARA	German Council for Computing Machines

DARE	Documentation Automated Retrieval Equipment
DARES	Data Analysis and Reduction System
DART	Daily Automatic Rescheduling Technique
DART	Data Analysis Recording Tape
DAS	Data Acquisition System
DAS	Datatron Assembly System
DAS	Digital Analog Simulator
DASD	Direct Access Storage Device
DASK	Danish Computer
DASK ALGOL	Danish version of ALGOL
DAT	Dynamic Address Translation
DATAC	Data Analog Computer
DATACOL	Data Collection System
DATACOM	Data Communications
DATAGEM	Data File Generator
DATAK	Data Acquisition Programming Language (DEC)
DATANAL	Interpretive Language
DATANET	General Electric Communications Computer
DATAPLUS	Information Retrieval Programming Language
DATA-TEXT	Programming Language
DATRIX	Direct Access to Reference Information
DAVI	Department of Audio Visual Instruction

DA Z002	Supervisory System
DB	Debit
DB	Decibel
D-B	Decimal-to-Binary
DBL	Metacompiler
DBM	Data Base Management System
DBMS	Data Base Management System
DBUG	Debugging Program
DC	Data Channel
DC	Data Check
DC	Data Collection
DC	Data Communications
DC	Decimal Classification
DC	Device Control Character
DC	Dewey Decimal Classification
DC	Digital Comparator
DC	Digital Computer
DC	Direct Current
DC	Disc Controller
DC	Display Code
DC	Display Console
DCA	Defense Communications Agency
DCA	Digital Computer Association
DCA	Direction Center Active
DCA	Diversified Computer Applications
DCB	Data Control Block
DCC	Data Communication Channel

DCCU	Data Communications Control Unit
DCD	Dynamic Computer Display
DCDS	Digital Control Design System
DCL	Digital Computer Laboratory
DCMT	Document
DCP	Data Communication Processor
DCP	Digital Computer Programming
DCR	Data Conversion Receiver
DCR	Data Coordinator and Retriever
DCR	Design Change Recommendation
DCR	Detail Condition Register
DCR	Digital Conversion Receiver
DCS	Data Communication System
DCS	Data Communications Subsystem
DCS	Data Control Services
DCS	Digital Command System
DCS	Digital Communication System
DCS	Direct-Couple Operating System (IBM)
DCS	Distributed Computer System
DCTL	Direct-Coupled Transistor Logic
DCU	Data Control Unit
DD	Data Definition
DD	Decimal Divide
DD	Dewey Decimal
DD	Digital Data
DD	Digital Display

DDA	Digital Differential Analyzer
DDAS	Digital Data Acquisition System
DDC	Defense Documentation Center
DDC	Digital Display Converter
DDC	Direct Digital Control
DDCE	Digital Data Conversion Equipment
DDCS	Digital Data Calibration System
DDD	Direct Distance Dialing
DDG	Digital Data Generator
DDG	Digital Display Generator
DDGE	Digital Display Generator Element
DDL	Digital System Design Language
DDM	Digital Display Makeup
DDOCE	Digital Data Output Conversion Equipment
DDP	Digital Data Processor
DDPU	Digital Data Processing Unit
DDS	Data Display Subsystem
DDS	Digital Display Scope
DDT	Digital Data Transmission
DDT	Digital Data Transmitter
DDT	Digital Debugging Tape
DDT	Dynamic Debugging Technique
DDTE	Digital Data Terminal Equipment
DE	Decision Element
DE	Design Engineering
DE	Device End

DE	Digital Element
DE	Display Element
DE	Display Equipment
DE	Division Entry
DEACON	Direct English Access and Control
DEAL	Decision Evaluation and Logic
DEBUT	Debugging System (UNIVAC M-460)
DEC	Decimal
DEC	Decision
DEC	Digital Equipment Corporation
DECADE	Digital Equipment Corporation's Automatic Design System
DECI	One-tenth
DECOM	Compiler for Reduction and Separation of Space Data
DECR	Decrement
DECUS	Digital Equipment Computer Users Society
DEDUCOM	Deductive Communicator
DEE	Digital Evaluation Equipment
DEFT	Dynamic Error-Free Transmission
DEG	Degree
DEL	Delay
DEL	Delete
DEL	Delete Character
DEN	Density
DENS	Density
DEPI	Differential Equation Pseudo Code Interpreter

DES	Design
DES	Differential Equation Solver
DES	Digital Expansion System
DESC	Digital Equation Solving Computer
DESCR	Description
DESK	Conversational Problem-Solving Language (DEC)
DET	Determinant
DETAB	Decision Table
DETAP	Decision Table Processor
DETOC	Decision Table to COBOL
DETRAN	Decision Translator
DEUA	Digitronics Equipment Users Association
DEUCE	Digital Electronic Universal Calculating Engine
DEV	Development
DEXAN	Digital Experimental Airborne Navigator
DF	Decimal Fraction
DF	Direct Flow
DF	Disk File
DFL	Display Formatting Language
DG	Differential Generator
DG	Diode Gate
DGBC	Digital Geoballistic Computer
DGC	Data General Corporation
DGNL	Diagonal
DGS	Data Gathering System

D-H	Decimal-to-Hexadecimal
DHE	Data Handling Equipment
DI	Data Input
DI	Digital Input
DIA	Diameter
DIAL	Display Interactive Assembly Language (DEC)
DIAL	Drum Interrogation, Alteration and Loading System (Honeywell)
DIALGOL	Dialect of ALGOL
DIALOG	Computer Graphics Programming System
DIAMAG	On-line Extension of ALGOL
DIAN	Digital Analog Simulator
DIANA	Digital Computer
DIAS	Dynamic Inventory Analysis System
DIBOL	Digital's (DEC) Business Oriented Language
DICT	Dictionary
DICTATOR	Automatic Coding System
DID	Datamation Industry Directory
DID	Digital Information Display
DIDAD	Digital Data Display
DIDAP	Digital Data Processor
DI/DO	Data Input/Data Output
DIG COMP	Digital Computer
DIGITAR	Digital Airborne Computer
DIG TRNR	Digital Trainer (UNIVAC)
DIM	Dimension

DIMATE	Depot-Installed Maintenance Automatic Test Equipment
DIO	Diode
DIOB	Digital Input/Output Buffer
DIP	Display Information Processor
DIPS	Development Information Processing System
DIS-68	Programming Language for Russian Computers
DISAC	Digital Simulator and Computer
DISADEC	Danish Computer
DISP	Display
DISTRIBUTAPE	Distributing Tape Computer (Litton)
DITRAN	Diagnostic FORTRAN (University of Wisconsin)
DIVA	Digital Input Voice Answer-back
DIVOT	Digital-to-Voice Translator
DL	Data Link
DL	Diode Logic
DL/1	Data Language/1
DLC	Duplex Line Control
DLE	Data Link Escape
DLP	Data Listing Programs
DLSC	Defense Logistics Services Center
DLT	Data Loop Transceiver
DLT	Decision Logic Table
DLY	Delay
DM	Data Management
DM	Data Manager

DM	Decimal Multiply
DM	Design Manual
DMA	Direct Memory Access
DMED	Digital Message Entry Device
DMR	Dynamic Modular Replacement
DMS	Data Management Service
DMS	Data Management System
DMV	German Federation of Mathematicians
DN	Decimal Number
DNC	Direct Numerical Control
DNIPRO	Russian Digital Computer
DO	Data Output
D-O	Decimal-to-Octal
DO	Digital Output
DOC	Data Optimizing Computer
DOC	Decimal-to-Octal Conversion
DOC	Document
DOCS	Disk Oriented Computer System
DOCUS	Display-Oriented Computer Usage System
DOD	Department of Defense
DODCI	Department of Defense Computer Institute
DODDAC	Department of Defense Damage Assessment Center
DOF	Degree of Freedom
DOFACS	Depreciation of Fixed Assets System

DO/IT	Digital Output/Input Translator
DOL	Display-Oriented Language
DOPE	Assembler/Compiler (DISAC Computer)
DOPIC	Documentation Of Programs In Core (Compress)
DOPS	Digital Optical Projection System
DORIS	Direct Order Recording and Invoicing System
DOS	Digital Operation System
DOS	Disk Operating System
DOS/360	Disk Operating System (IBM System/360)
DOW COMPILER	Automatic Coding System
DP	Data Processing
DP	Disk Pack
DP	Drum Processor
DP	Dynamic Programming
DPA	Data Processing Activities
DPB	Data Processing Branch
DPC	Data Processing Center
DPC	Data Processing Central
DPC	Direct Program Control
DP&C	Data Processing Computation
DPD	Data Processing Department
DPD	Data Processing Division
DPD	Digit Plane Driver
DPE	Data Processing Equipment

DPF	Data Processing Facility
DPG	Data Processing Group
DPG	Datatrol Patch Generator
DPG	Digital Pattern Generator
DPG	German Physical Society
DPI	Data Processing Installation
DPM	Data Processing Machine
DPM	Data Processing Manager
DPM	Documents Per Minute
DPMA	Data Processing Management Association
DPMOAP	Society of DP Machine Operators and Programmers
DPMS	Data Project Management System
DPS	Data Processing Service
DPS	Data Processing Subsystem
DPS	Data Processing System
DPS	Disc Programming System
DPS	Document Processing System
DPSA	Data Processing Supplies Association
DPSS	Data Processing Sub-System
DPSS	Data Processing System Simulator
DPU	Data Processing Unit
DQC	Data Quality Control
DR	Data Recorder
DR	Data Reduction
DR	Drive

DR	Drum
D/R	Direct
DRC	Data Reduction Compiler
DRI	Data Reduction Interpreter
DRO	Destructive Read-Out
DRO	Digital Readout
DROS	Disk Resident Operating System
DRUCO I	Interpretative Floating Decimal System
DS	Data Scanning
DS	Data Set
DS	Decimal Subtract
DS	Define Storage
DS	Define Symbol
DS	Disk Storage
DS	Drum Storage
D&S	Display and Storage
DSC	Document Service Center
DSCB	Data-Set Control Block
DSCS	Desk Side Computer System
DSD	Digital System Design
DSE	Data Storage Equipment
DSE	Data Systems Engineering
DSIR	Department of Scientific Industrial Research
DSL	Data Set Label
DSL	Data Structures Language

DSL	Digital Simulation Language
DSMG	Designated Systems Management Group
DSN	Data System News
DSU	Disk Storage Unit
DSW	Data Status Word
DT	Data Translator
DT	Data Transmission
DT	Digital Technique
D/T	Disk-Tape
DT	Down Time
DTB	Decimal to Binary
DTF	Define The File
DTG	Display Transmission Generator
DTI	Department of Trade and Industry
DTIB	Decision Table Information Bulletin
DTL	Diode Transistor Logic
DTP	Directory Tape Processor
DTR	Daily Transaction Reporting
DTS	Data Transmission System
DTU	Digital Tape Unit
DTU	Digital Transmission Unit
DTUTF	Digital Tape Unit Tape Facility
D/TV	Digital to Television
DUAL	Dynamic Universal Assembly Language
DUMBO	Automatic Programming System

DUNS	Data Universal Numbering System
DUO	Datatron Users Organization
DUP	Duplication
DUT	Device Under Test
DVM	Digital Volt Meter
DVM	Displaced Virtual Machine
DX	Duplex
DYANA	Dynamics Analyzer (Programming Language)
DYN	Dynamic
DYNAMO	Dynamic Model (a simulation language)
DYNASAR	Dynamic Systems Analyzer (GE)
DYSAC	Digitally Simulated Analog Computer
DYSEAC	Second Standards Electronic Automatic Computer (NBS)
DYSTAC	Dynamic Storage Analog Computer
DYSTAL	Dynamic Storage Allocation Language

E

E	Error
E	Real Constant—FORTRAN
E-364	Translation Program
EA	Effective Address
EAG	Equipment Advisory Group
EAI	Electronics Associates, Inc.
EAM	Electrical Accounting Machine
EAM	Electronic Accounting Machinery
EAM	Electronic-Automatic Machine
EAROM	Electronically Alterable Read-Only Memory
EASCON	Electronics and Aerospace Systems Convention
EASE	Electrical Automatic Support Equipment
EASE II	Engineering Automatic System for Solving Equations
EASI	Electrical Accounting for the Security Industry (IBM)
EASIAC	Pseudo Computer (University of Michigan, MIDAC)
EASL	Engineering Analysis and Simulation Language
EASTCON	Electronics and Aerospace Systems Technical Convention
EASY	Efficient Assembly System
EASY FOX	Assembly System (JOHNNIAC—Rand Corp.)

EAX	Electronic Automatic Exchange
EBCDIC	Extended Binary Coded Decimal Interchange Code
EC	Electronic Calculators
EC	Engineering Change
EC	Error Correcting
ECAP	Electronic Circuit Analysis Program
ECARS	Electronic Coordinatograph and Readout System
ECB	Event Control Block
ECC	Electronic Components Conference
ECC	Executive Computer Concepts
ECCANE	East Coast Conference on Aerospace and Navigational Electronics
ECHO	Electronic Computing Hospital Oriented (Users Group)
ECL	Equipment Component List
ECM	Electronic Counter Measures
ECMA	European Computer Manufacturers Association
ECN	Engineering Change Notice
ECO	Engineering Change Order
ECP	Engineering Change Proposal
ECP	Executive Control Program
ECPI	Electronic Computer Programming Institute
ECS	Executive Control System
ECS	Extended Core Storage
ED	Error Detecting

ED	Expanded Display
ED	External Device
EDA	Electronic Differential Analyzer
EDA	Electronic Digital Analyzer
EDAC	Error Detection and Correction
EDB	Educational Data Bank
EDC	Electronic Desk Calculator
EDC	Electronic Digital Computer
EDC	Error Detection and Correction
EDCOM	Editor and Compiler
EDCW	External Device Control Word
EDGE	Electronic Data Gathering Equipment
EDOS	Extended Disk Operating System
EDP	Electronic Data Processing
EDPC	Electronic Data Processing Center
EDPE	Electronic Data Processing Equipment
EDPEO	Electronic Data Processing Equipment Office
EDPI	Electronic Data Processing Institute
EDP/IR	EDP Industry and Market Report
EDPM	Electronic Data Processing Machine
EDPS	Electronic Data Processing System
EDRS	Engineering Data Retrieval System
EDSAC	Electronic Delay Storage Automatic Computer
EDST	Elastic Diaphragm Switch Technology (IBM)

EDU	Electronic Display Unit
EDUCOM	Interuniversity Communications Council
EDVAC	Electronic Discrete Variable Analog Computer
EDVAC	Electronic Discrete Variable Automatic Computer
EE	Electrical Engineer
EE	Evaluation Engineering
EEA	Electronic Engineering Association (Great Britain)
EELM	English Electric—Leo—Marconi
EGDON	Operating System (KDF9 Computer)
EGPS	Extended General Purpose Simulator (NEC)
EHF	Extremely High Frequency
EIA	Electronic Industries Association
EIAC	Electronic Industries Association of Canada
EIC	Engineering Institute of Canada
EIN	Education Information Network
EJCC	Eastern Joint Computer Conference
ELBIT	Elbit Computers Ltd. (computer manufacturer in Israel)
ELECOM	Electronic Computer
ELEM	Element
ELF	Extensible Language Facility
ELI	Equitable Life Interpreter
ELIZA	Text Processing Language

ELLIOTT	Elliott Automation
ELP	English Language Test Procedure
EM	Extensible Machine
EMA	Extended Mercury Autocoder
EMI-70	Educational Management and Instructional System-70
EMIS	Educational Management Information System
EMP	Electromechanical Power
EMR	Electro-Mechanical Research
EMR	Executive Management Responsibility
END	End of Data
ENG	Engineering
ENGR	Engineer
ENIAC	Electronic Numerical Integrator and Calculator
ENT	Entry
EO	Elementary Operation
EO	Engineering Order
EO	European Office
EOA	End of Address
EOB	End of Block
EOD	End of Data
EOF	End of File
EOJ	End of Job
EOL	End of Life
EOL	Expression Oriented Language (Symbol Manipulation Programming Language)

EOLT	End of Logical Tape
EOM	End of Message
EOP	End of Program
EOR	End of Record
EOR	End of Reel
EOS	Electro-Optical System
EOT	End of Tape
EOT	End of Transmission
EOV	End of Volume
EP	Elongated Punch
EP	Entry Point
EP	Extended Performance (IBM System/4 Pi)
EP	Extra Precision
EPAM	Elementary Perceiver and Memorizer (University of California)
EPC	Electronic Program Control
EPOS	Czechoslovakian Computer
EPS	Equilibrium Problem Solver
EPU	Electrical Power Unit
EQ	Equal to (FORTRAN)
EQP	Equipment
EQU	Equate
ERA	Electronic Reading Automation
ERA	Engineering Research Associates
ERFPI	Extended Range Floating Point Interpretive System
ERIC	Educational Research Information Center

ERMA	Electronic Recording Machine Accounting (GE)
ERMETH	Swiss Electronic Computer
ERNIE	Electronic Random Numbering and Indicating Equipment
ERR	Error
ERX	Electronic Remote Switching
ES	Electromagnetic Storage
ES	Electronic Switch
ESC	Escape Character (Teletypewriter)
ESCAPE	Expansion Symbolic Compiling Assembly Program for Engineering
ESD	Electrostatic Storage Deflection
ESD	External Symbol Dictionary
ESE	Electrical Support Equipment
ESI	Engineering and Scientific Interpreter
ESMA	Electronic Sales and Marketing Association
ESONE	European Standards of Nuclear Electronics
ESP	Elliott Simulator Package
ESPOL	Executive System Problem Oriented Language
ESS	Electronic Switching System
EST	Electrostatic Storage Tube
EST	Estimate
ESW	Error Status Word
ET	Elapsed Time
ETAN	Yugoslav Committee for Electronics and Automation

ETC	Estimated Time of Completion
ETIM	Elapsed Time
ETL	Ending Tape Label
ETOS	Extended Tape Operating System
ETP	Electrical Tough Pitch
ETS	Electronic Telegraph System
ETX	End of Text Character
EUCLID	Experimental Use Computer, London Integrated Display
EUROCOMP	European Computing Congress
EUSEC	Engineering Societies of Western Europe and the United States
EVAL	Evaluation
EWCAS	Early Warning and Control Aircraft System
EX	Execute
EXCH	Exchange
EXCHANGE	CDC Users Group
EXCP	Except
EXDAMS	Extended Debugging and Monitoring System
EXEC	Executive
EXTSN	Extension

F

F	Farad
F	Feedback
F	Fixed
F	Frequency
FA	Fully Automatic
FAA	Federal Aviation Administration
FABLE	First ADAM Basic Language
FAC	Financial Administrative Control
FACI	First Article Configuration Inspection
FACIT	Swedish Digital Computer
FACOM	Japanese Computer Model Series of Fujitsu Ltd.
FACS	Flexible Accounting Control System
FACT	Factual Compiler
FACT	Foundation for Advanced Computer Technology
FACT	Fully Automatic Cataloging Technique
FACT	Fully Automatic Compiler-Translator
FACT	Fully Automatic Compiling Technique
FAD	Floating Add
FADAC	Field Artillery Digital Automatic Computer
FADP	Finnish Association for Data Processing

FAHQMT	Fully Automatic High-Quality Machine Translation
FAIR	Automatic Coding System
FALTRAN	FORTRAN to ALGOL Translator
FAM	Fast Auxiliary Memory
FAP	Financial Analysis Program
FAP	Floating Point Arithmetic Package
FAP	FORTRAN Assembly Program
FAR	Failure Analysis Report
FARET	Fast Reactor Test Facility
FARGO	Fourteen-o-one Automatic Report Generated Object
FASE	Fundamentally Analyzable Simplified English
FAST	Facility for Automatic Sorting and Testing
FAST	Fieldata Applications, Systems and Techniques
FAST	Federation of Scientific and Technical Associations of Milan, Italy
FAST	Flexible Algebraic Scientific Translator (NCR)
FAST	Formal Auto-indexing of Scientific Texts
FAST	Formula and Statement Translator
FAST	Four Address to SOAP Translator
FASTRAN	Fast FORTRAN II (Indiana University)
FAT	Formula Assembler Translator
FATAL	FADAC Automatic Test Analysis Language

FAX	Facsimile
FC	Ferrite Core
FC	File Code
FC	File Conversion
FC	Foot Candle
FC	Function Code
FCC	Federal Communications Commission
FCFS	First Come—First Served
FCFT	Fixed Cost—Fixed Time Estimate
FCL	Feedback Control Loop
FCL	Full Cycle Left
FCP	File Control Processor
FCPC	Fleet Computer Programming Center
FD	File Description
FD	Full Duplex
FDM	Frequency Division Multiplex
FDOS	Floppy Disk Operating System
FDP	Future Data Processors (DPMA)
FDX	Full Duplex
FE	Field Engineer
FEAT	Frequency of Every Allowable Term
FEI	Financial Executives Institute
FEP	Financial Evaluation Program
FERUT	Ferranti Machine at the University of Toronto
FET	Field-Effect Transistor
FF	Fixed Fee

F-F	Flip-Flop
FFL	First Financial Language
FFP	Firm Fixed Price
FGAA	Federal Government Accountants Association
FIB	FORTRAN Information Bulletin
FID	International Federation of Documentation
FIDAC	Film Input to Digital Automatic Computer
FIDACSYS	Programming Language
FIELDCOM	Field Computer
FIFO	First In—First Out
FIFO	Floating Input—Floating Output
FIG	Figure
FIIG	Federal Item Identification Guide
FINAC	Fast Interline Non-activate Automatic Control
FINAL	Financial Analysis Language
FIOT	FORTRAN Input-Output Package
FIRMS	Forecasting Information Retrieval of Management System
FIRST	Financial Information Reporting System
FIS	Field Information System
FIX	Fixed-Point
FJCC	Fall Joint Computer Conference
FL	Fault Location
FL	Floating Point

FL/1	Function Language 1
FLAC	Florida Automatic Computer
FLAIR	Automatic Programming System
FLAP	Flores Assembly Program
FLD	Field
FLDEC	Floating-Point Decimal
FLEXTRAN	Assembly Language
FLF	Fixed Length Field
FLF	Flip-Flop
FLG	Flag
FLIC	FORTRAN Converting Program
FLINT	Floating Interpretive Language
FLIP	Film Library Instantaneous Presentation
FLIP	Floating Indexed Point Arithmetic
FLIP	Floating Point Interpretive Program
FLIP	Pattern-directed String Processing Language
FLIT	Flexowriter Interrogation Tape
FLOCO	Programming Language
FLODAC	Fluid Operated Digital Automatic Computer (UNIVAC)
FLOGEN/F	Flowchart Generator/FORTRAN
FLOP	Floating Octal Point
FLOP	Programming Language
FLOPAK	Floating Point Programming System
FLOTRAN	Flowcharting FORTRAN

FLOW-MATIC	English-like language for business data processing
FLOWTRACE	Flowcharting Program
FLPL	FORTRAN List Processing Language
FLT	Fault Location Technology
FLT	Floating-Point
FM	File Maintenance
FM	Format
FM	Frequency Modulation
FMPS	FORTRAN IV Mathematical Programming System
FMPS	Functional Mathematical Programming System
FMT	Format
FNWF	Fleet Numerical Weather Facility
FOALBOL	Programming Language (combines FORTRAN, ALGOL and COBOL)
FOCAL	Formula Calculator (DEC)
FOCUS	Forum of Com-Share Users
FOIL	File Oriented Interpretive Language
FOPT	Fiber Optic Photo Transfer
FORAST	Programming Language (BRLESC and ORDVAC)
FORBLOC	FORTRAN Compiled Block Oriented Simulation Language
FORC	Formula Coder and Automatic Coding System
FORCE III	FORTRAN Conversational Environment

FOREMOST	Programming Language
FORGO	FORTRAN Load and Go System
FORMAC	Formula Manipulation Compiler
FORSOL	Compiler Language
FORTAB	Decision Table Processor (used with FORTRAN programs)
FORTOCOM	FORTRAN I Compiler
FOR-TO-GO	FORTRAN Load and Go System (University of Wisconsin)
FORTRAN	Formula Translation
FORTRAN I	Formula Translation I
FORTRAN II	Formula Translation II
FORTRAN IV	Formula Translation IV
FORTRAN V	Formula Translation V (UNIVAC 1100 series)
FORTRANSIT	FORTRAN and Internal Translator System
FORTRUNCIBLE	FORTRAN Style Runcible
FOSDIC	Film Optical Sensing Device for Input to Computers
FP	Feedback Positive
FP	File Protect
FP	Fixed-Point
FP	Fixed Price
FP	Floating-Point
FPC	Fixed Price Contract
FPI	Fixed Price Incentive
FPIF	Fixed Price—Incentive Fee

FPM	Feet Per Minute
FPP	Floating Point Processor
FPS	Feet Per second
FPS	Frames Per Second
FRED	Figure-Reader Electronic Device
FREQ	Frequency
FRINGE	File and Report Information Processing Generator
FRN	Floating Round
FS	Feasibility Study
FS	Federal Standard
FS	Field Service
FS	File Separator
FS	Floating Sign
FS	Full Scale
FS3	FORTRAN Operating System
FSB	Floating Subtract
FSDC	Federal Statistical Data Center
FSK	Frequency Shift Keying
FSL	Formal Semantic Language (M.I.T)
FT	Full Time
FT	Functional Test
FTS	Federal Telecommunications System
FTS	Free-Time System (GE/PAC computers)
FUJITSU	Fujitsu Limited (Japanese computer manufacturer)

FUN	Function
FUSE	IBM Computer Users Group
FWA	First Word Address
FWL	Fixed Word Length
FX	Fixed Point
FX	Foreign Exchange
FY	Fiscal Year

G

G	Giga
GAM	Graphic Access Method (IBM)
GAMA	Graphics Assisted Management Application
GAMM	German Association for Applied Mathematics and Mechanics
GAN	Generating and Analyzing Networks
GAP	General Assembly Program
GAR	Growth Analysis and Review
GARGOYLE	Compiler Language (Norwegian Defense Research Est., Kjeller, Norway)
GASP	General Activity Simulation Program
GASP	Generalized Academic Simulation Program
GASP	Graphic Applications Subroutine Package
GASS	Generalized Assembly System
GAT	Generalized Algebraic Translator
GAT	Georgetown Automatic Translator
GATB	General Aptitude Test Battery
GATE	Generalized Algebraic Translator Extended
GAULTRAN	French Programming Language
GC	Gigacycle
GC	Guidance Computer

GCAP	Generalized Circuit Analysis Program
GCD	Greatest Common Divisor
GCMA	Government Contract Management Association of America
GCPS	Gigacycles Per Second
GCT	Greenwich Civil Time
GDE	Ground Data Equipment
GDG	Generation Data Group
GDMS	Generalized Data Management System
GE	General Electric Company
GE	Germanium
GE	Greater Than or Equal to (FORTRAN)
GEC	G. E. C. Computers and Automation, Ltd. (British computer manufacturer)
GECOM	Generalized Compiler
GECOS	General Comprehensive Operating Supervisor
GEEP	General Electric Electronic Processor
GEESE	General Electric's Electronic System Evaluator
GEFRC	General File/Record Control
GEIR	Danish Computer
GE/MAC	General Electric Measurement And Control
GEMS	General Education Management System
GEN	Generate

GEN	Generator
GENL	General
GEORGE	Digital Computer (Argonne National Laboratory)
GEORGE	General Organizational Environment
GEOTECH AUTOMATIC	Geotechnical Automatic Chart Reader
GE/PAC	General Electric Process Automation Computer
GERTS	General Electric Remote Terminal Supervisor
GET	General Electric Computer Users Group
GE/TAC	General Electric Telemetering And Control
GETEL	General Electric Test Engineering Language
GETEL	General Electric Training Operational Logic
GEVIC	General Electric Variable Increment Computer
GFE	Government Furnished Equipment
GHCP	Georgia Hospital Computer Group
GIANT	Genealogical Information and Name Tabulating System
GIF	Gulf IT to FORTRAN Translator
GIFS	Generalized Interrelated Flow Simulation
GIFT	General Internal FORTRAN Translator

GIGO	Garbage In—Garbage Out
GIM	Generalized Information Management Language
GIOC	Generalized Input/Output Controller
GIPS	Ground Information Processing System
GIPSY	Generalized Information Processing System
GIRL	Graph Information Retrieval Language
GIRLS	Generalized Information Retrieval and Listing System
GIS	Generalized Information System (IBM)
GIS	Geoscience Information Society
GIT	Graph Isomorphism Tester (Columbia University)
GLAD	General Ledger Account Distribution
GLEAN	Graphic Layout and Engineering Aid Method (IBM)
GLOTRAC	Global Tracking
GM	Group Mark
GMAP	General Macro Assembly Program
GMS	General Maintenance System
GMT	General Machine Test
GMT	General Mean Time
GMT	Greenwich Mean Time
GOAL	Ground Operations Aerospace Language
GOCI	General Operator-Computer Interaction

GOE	Ground Operation Equipment
GOL	General Operating Language
GOLD	Graphic On-Line Language
GOPAC	Graphical Output Circuit Analysis Program
GOTRAN	Load and Go FORTRAN (IBM)
GP	Gang Punch
GP	General Purpose
GP	Generalized Programming
GPA	General Purpose Analysis
GPATS	General Purpose Automatic Test System
GPC	General Purpose Computer
GPCP	General Purpose Contouring Program
GPDC	General Purpose Digital Computer
GPDS	General Purpose Display System
GPGL	General Purpose Graphic Language
GPL	General Purpose Language
GPL	Generalized Programming Language
GPLAN	Generalized Data Base Planning System
GPLP	General Purpose Linear Programming
GPM	General Purpose Macrogenerator (Atlas 2)
GPMS	General Purpose Microprogram Simulator
GPO	General Purpose Macrogenerator
GPO	Government Printing Office
GPS	General Problem Solver

GPSS	General Purpose Systems Simulator (IBM)
GPX	Generalized Programming Extended (UNIVAC LARC)
GR	Group
GRACE	Graphic Arts Composing Equipment
GRAD	Graduate Resume Accumulation and Distribution
GRADB	Generalized Remote Access Data Base
GRADS	Generalized Remote Access Data Base System
GRAF	Graphic Additions to FORTRAN
GRANITE	Special Purpose Russian Computer
GRAPDEN	Graphic Data Entry Unit
GRASP	Graphic Service Program
GRATIS	Generation, Reduction, And Training Input System
GRED	Generalized Random Extract Device
GRID	Graphical Interactive Display
GRIN	Graphical Input
GRP	Group
GRS	Generalized Retrieval System
GRUB	Grocery Update and Billing
GSA	General Services Administration
GSFS	Goddard Space Flight Center
GSL	Generation Strategy Language
GSL	Generalized Simulation Language
GSP	General Simulation Program (programming language)

GSS	Graphic Service System
GSSC	Ground Support Simulation Computer
GT	Game Theory
GT	Greater Than (FORTRAN)
GTD	Graphic Tablet Display
GUIDE	Computer Users Association (IBM)
GULP	General Utility Library Program

H

H	Half-word
H	Halt
H	Hardware
H	Henry (unit of conductance)
H	Hexadecimal
H	Honeywell Information Systems, Inc.
HA	Half Adder
HABEAS	Structural Dynamics Analysis System
HAL	Highly Automated Logic
HAL	Honeywell Author Language
HALSIM	Hardware Logic Simulator
HAMPSHIRE CCC	Coordinate Conversion Computer
HAMPSHIRE TRTDS	Hampshire Theodolite Real Time Display System
HARP	Hitachi Arithmetic Processor
HARTRAN	Hardwell FORTRAN
HASP	Houston Automatic Spooling Priority System
HAYSTAQ	Information Retrieval System
HB	Handbook
H-B	Hexadecimal-to-Binary
H/C	Hand Carry
HC	Hard Copy
HC	Heuristic Concepts
HC	Hybrid Computer

HCSS	Hospital Computer Sharing System
HD	Density
HD	Half Duplex
H-D	Hexadecimal-to-Decimal
HDDS	High-Density Data System
HDOC	Handy Dandy Orbital Computer
HDR	Header
HDW	Hardware
HDX	Half Duplex
HE	Handling Duplex
HEC	Hollerith Electronic Computer
HEEP	Highway Engineering Exchange Program (Users Group)
HELP	Highly Extendable Language Processor
HEW	Department of Health, Education and Welfare
HEX	Hexadecimal
HF	High Frequency
HFS	Human Factor Society
HI	High
HIDM	High Information Delta Modulation
HIIS	Honeywell Institute for Information Science
HIS	Honeywell Information Systems, Inc.
HISI	Honeywell Information Systems, Inc.
HITACHI	Hitachi, Ltd. (Japanese computer manufacturer)

HL	High Level
HLD	Hold
HLL	Higher Level Language
HLT	Halt
HMSS	Hospital Management Systems Society
HOI	HYTRAN Operations Interpreter
HOP	Hybrid Operating Program
HP	Hewlett-Packard Company
HP	Horse Power
HS	Half Subtractor
HS	High Speed
HSD	High Speed Data
HSDA	High Speed Data Acquisition
HSK	Housekeeping
HSL	HYTRAN Simulation Language
HSM	High Speed Memory
HSP	High Speed Printer
HSR	High Speed Reader
HSR	High Speed Rewind
HSRO	High Speed Repetitive Operation
HSS	High Speed Storage
HT	Half Time
HTSS	Honeywell Time-Sharing System
HV	Hardware Virtualizer
HV	High Voltage
HYCOL	Hybrid Computer Link

HYCOTRAN	Hybrid Computer Translator
HYDAC	Hybrid Digital-Analog Computer (EAI)
HYPER	Hypertape
HYTRAN	Hybrid Programming Language
HZ	Hertz (one cycle per second)

I

I	Current
I	Indicator
I	Input
I	Inverter
IA	Indirect Addressing
IAC	International Algebraic Compiler
IACP	International Association of Computer Programmers
IADIC	Integration Analog-to-Digital Converter
IAG	IFIP Administrative Data Processing Group
IAL	International Algorithmic Language
IAL	Investment Analysis Language
IAM	Interactive Algebraic Manipulation
IAO	Internal Automation Operation
IAS	Immediate Access Storage
IAS	Institute for Advanced Study
IAS	Interactive Applications Supervisor
IASA	Insurance Accounting and Statistical Association
IAT	International Accountants Society, Inc.
IAT	Institute for Advanced Technology
IAT	Institute of Automatics and Telemechanics (U.S.S.R.)

IAW	In Accordance With
IBFI	International Business Forms Industries
IBG	Interblock Gap
IBI	Intergovernmental Bureau for Informatics
IBM	International Business Machines Corporation
IBS	Institute for Basic Standards
IC	Input Circuit
IC	Instruction Counter
IC	Integrated Circuit
IC	Interface Control
I & C	Installation and Checkout
ICA	Industrial Communications Association
ICA	International Communication Association
ICC	International Computation Centre (Rome, Italy)
ICCP	Institute for Certification of Computer Professionals
ICE	Input Checking Equipment
ICE	Integrated Electronic Components
ICEM	International Council for Educational Media
ICES	Integrated Civil Engineering System
ICETRAN	ICES-FORTRAN Programming Language of ICES
ICG	Interactive Computer Graphics

ICIP	International Conference on Information Processing
ICL	Incoming Line
ICL	International Computers Ltd. (British computer firm)
ICM	Integrated Search Memory (UNIVAC)
ICP	International Computer Programs
ICRH	Institute for Computer Research in the Humanities (New York University)
ICS	Inland Computer Service
ICS	Institute for Computing Sciences
ICS	Italian Computer Society
ICSU	International Council of Scientific Unions
ICT	Institute of Computer Technology
ICT	International Computers and Tabulators Limited (British computer manufacturer)
ID	Identification
ID	Identifier
I/D	Instruction/Data
ID	Item Description
IDABEE	Institute of Defense Analysis Compiler
IDAS	Information Displays Automatic Drafting System
IDEEA	Information and Data Exchange Experimental Activities
IDEP	Interagency Data Exchange Program
IDF	Integrated Data File

IDIOT	Instrumentation Digital On-Line Transcriber
IDP	Industrial Data Processing
IDP	Input Data Processor
IDP	Integrated Data Presentation
IDP	Integrated Data Processing
IDPC	Integrated Data Processing Center
IDPI	International Data Processing Institute
IDR	Industrial Data Reduction
IDS	Integrated Data Store
IE	Industrial Engineering
IEC	Integrated Electronic Components
IEC	International Electrotechnical Commission
IEE	Institution of Electrical Engineers (now IEEE)
IEE	Institution of Electrical Engineers (England)
IEEE	Institute of Electrical and Electronics Engineers
IEEETEC	IEEE Transactions on Electronic Computers
I/F	Interface
IFAC	International Federation of Automatic Control
IFAM	Information Systems for Associative Memories
IFB	Invitation for Bid

IFCS	International Federation of Computer Sciences
IFD	International Federation for Documentation
IFGL	Initial File Generation Language
IFIP	International Federation for Information Processing
IFIPC	International Federation for Information Processing Congress
IFIPS	International Federation of Information Processing Societies
IFORS	International Federation of Operating Research Societies
IGFET	Insulated-Gate Field-Effect Transistor
IGS	Integrated Graphics System
IIA	Information Industry Association
IIS	Institute of Information Scientists
IITRAN	Illinois Institute of Technology Programming Language
IJCAI	International Joint Conference on Artificial Intelligence
IL	Incorrect Length
IL	Intermediate Language
ILC	Instruction Length Code
ILJM	*Illinois Journal of Mathematics*
ILLIAC	Illinois Integrator and Automatic Computer (University of Illinois)
ILLIAD	Illinois Algorithmic Decoder (Southern Illinois University)

ILLINET	Computer Communications Network at the University of Illinois
ILM	Information-Logic Machine
ILP	Intermediate Language Processor
IM	Industri-Mathematatik (Swedish software firm)
IM	Instrumentation
IMC	International Micrographic Congress
IMITAC	Image Input to Automatic Computers
IMM	Institute of Mathematics Machines (Poland)
IMP	Implementation Language
IMP	Industrial Management Program
IMP	Interface Message Processor
IMP	Intrinsic Multiprocessing
IMPACT	Inventory Management Program and Control Techniques System (IBM)
IMPRESS	Interdisciplinary Machine Processing for Research and Education in the Social Sciences
IMRADS	Information Management Retrieval and Dissemination System
IMS	Industrial Management Society
IMS	Industrial Mathematics Society
IMS	Information Management System
IMS	Institute of Management Sciences
IMS	Institute of Mathematical Statistics
IMS	Instructional Management System
IMS	Inventory Management and Simulator

IN	Input
I/N	Item Number
INC.	Incorporated
INCOMEX	International Computer Exhibition
INCR	Increase
INCUM	Indiana Computer Users Meeting
IND	Indicator
INF	Information
INFO	Information
INFO	Information Network and File Organization
INFOL	Information Oriented Language
INFRAL	Information Retrieval Automatic Language
INHIB	Inhibit
INIS	International Nuclear Information System
INSCAN	Syntax-Directed Language Processor
INST	Instruction
INST	Instrument
INSTR	Instruction
INT	Initial
INT	Integer
INTEL	Intelligence
INTER	Interference
INTER	Interrupt
INTERCARD	Interpreter-Compiler
INTERCOM	Automatic Coding System

INTERCOM	Intercommunication
INTERFOR	Interpretive Programming System
INTERKAMA	International Congress and Exhibition of Measuring Instruments and Automation
INTERP	Interpolation
INTIPS	Integrated Information Processing System
INTRAN	Input Translator
INTREX	Information Transfer Experiments (M.I.T.)
I/O	Input-Output
I-O	Input-Output
IO	Interpretive Operation
IOB	Input-Output Buffer
IOC	Input-Output Controller
IOCS	Input-Output Control System
IOM	Input-Output Multiplexer
IOMUX	Input-Output Multiplexer
IOP	Input-Output Processor
IOPKG	Input-Output Package
IOPS	Input-Output Programming System
IOR	Input-Output Register
IOS	Input-Output Selector
IOS	Input-Output Supervisor
IOS	International Organization for Standardization
IOTA	Information Overload Testing Apparatus

IP	Information Processing
IP	Initial Point
IP	Item Processing
IPA	Information Processing Association
IPAI	Information Processing Association of Israel
IPC	Industrial Process Control
IPC	Information Processing Center
IPC	Information Processing Code
IPE	Information Processing Equipment
IPI	Individually Prescribed Instruction
IPL	Information Processing Language
IPL	Initial Program Loading
IPL-IV	Information Processing Language IVth Version
IPL-V	Information Processing Language Vth Version
IPL-TS	Information Processing Language—Time Sharing
IPM	Impulses Per Minute
IPM	Institute for Practical Mathematics (Germany)
IPM	Interruptions Per Minute
IPO	Installation Planning Order
IPS	Inches Per Second
IPS	Interruptions Per Second
IPSOC	Information Processing Society of Canada
IPSSB	Information Processing Systems Standards Board

IR	Information Retrieval
IRDP	Information Retrieval Data Bank
IRE	Institute of Radio Engineers
IRG	Interrecord Gap
IRL	Information Retrieval Language
IRS	Information Retrieval System
IRSIA	Institute for the Enouragement of Scientific Research in Industry (Belgium)
ISA	Instrument Society of America
ISALIS	Indian Society for Automation and Information Sciences
ISAM	Indexed Sequential Access Method
ISAM	Integrated Switching And Multiplexing
ISAR	Information Storage and Retrieval
ISC	Information Society of Canada
ISDS	Integrated Ship Design System
ISEQ	Input Sequence Checking
ISI	Institute for Scientific Information
ISI	Internally Specified Index
ISIS	Internal State Information System (Colorado)
ISIS	Version of JOSS (language)
ISJM	*Israeli Journal of Mathematics*
ISK	Insert Storage Key
ISL	Information Search Language
ISL	Information System Language
ISL	Instructional Systems Language

ISL	Interactive Simulation Language
ISM	Information Systems for Management
ISME	Industrial, Scientific, and Medical Equipment
ISO	Individual System Operation
ISO	International Standards Organization
ISP	Italian Society of Physics
ISR	Information Storage and Retrieval
ISS	Information Storage System
ISS	Input Subsystem
ISSN	International Standard Serial Number
IST	Information Science and Technology
IST	Integrated System Test
ISTIM	Interchange of Scientific and Technical Information in Machine Language
ISU	Interface Switching Unit
ISU	International Scientific Union
ISWIM	Programming Language
IT	Input Translator
IT	Internal Translator (language)
IT	Item Transfer
ITA	International Tape Association
ITB	Invitation to Bid
ITCC	International Technical Communications Conference
ITE	Institute of Telecommunication Engineers

ITE	Institute of Traffic Engineers
ITF	Interactive Terminal Facility
ITIRC	IBM Technical Information Retrieval Center
ITN	International Telecomputer Network Corporation
ITP	Individual Training Program
ITPS	Integrated Teleprocessing System (IBM)
ITS	Invitation To Send
ITT	International Telephone & Telegraph Company
ITU	International Telecommunication Union
ITV	Instructional Television
IUPAP	International Union of Pure and Applied Physics
IV	Inverter
IVERSON	Programming Language
IVY	Programming Language
IX	Index

J

J	Jack
J	Joule
JA	Jump Address
JACC	Joint Automatic Control Conference
JACM	*Journal of the Association for Computing Machinery*
JADE	Japan Area Defense Environment
JAEDS	New Jersey Association for Educational Data Systems
JAPT	*Journal of Approximation Theory*
JASIS	*Journal of the American Society for Information Science*
JAUS	*Journal of the Australian Mathematical Society*
JAZ	Interpretive Routine
JBMMA	Japanese Business Machine Makers Association
JCC	Joint Communications Center
JCC	Joint Computer Conference
JCL	Job Control Language
JCP	Job Control Program
JCMT	*Journal of Combinatorial Theory*
JCSS	*Journal of Computer and System Sciences*
JDA	Job Description Card
JDM	*Journal of Data Management*

JECC	Japanese Electronic Computer Company
JEDEC	Joint Electron Device Engineering Council
JEIDA	Japan Electronic Industry Industry Development Association
JEIPAC	Japan Electronic Industry Development Association
JEMC	Joint Engineering Management Conference
JIB	Job Information Block
JIB	JOVIAL Information Bulletin
JK	Joint Industry Conference
JIMS	*Journal of the Indian Mathematical Society*
JIP	Joint Input Processing
JIS	Japanese Industrial Standards
JISC	Japanese Industrial Standards Committee
JLMS	*Journal of the London Mathematical Society*
JMA	Japan Microphotography Association
JMKU	*Journal of Mathematics of Kyoto University*
JMPY	*Journal of Mathematical Physics*
JMSJ	*Journal of the Mathematical Society of Japan*
JO	Job Order
JOHNNIAC	Johns (von Neumann) Integrator and Automatic Computer

JOLA	*Journal of Library Automation*
JOSL	User-Oriented, Conversational Programming Language
JOSS	JOHNNIAC Open-Shop System (Rand Corp.)
JOVIAL	Jules' Own Version of the International Algebraic Language
JPL	Jet Propulsion Laboratory
JPW	Job Processing Word
JSC	Johnson Spacecraft Center
JSLG	*Journal of Symbolic Logic*
JSS	Job Shop Simulator (IBM)
JSSPG	Job Shop Simulation Program Generator
JTS	JOVIAL for Time-Sharing
JUG	Joint User's Group
JUKEBOX	Missile Firing Data Computer (NAA)

K

K	Kilo (1024 in decimal notation)
K5	Automatic Coding System (UNIVAC LARC Computer)
KAEDS	Keystone Association for Educational Data Systems
KB	Keyboard
KB	Kilobits
KBS	Kilobits per Second
KC	Kilocycle (one thousand cycles per second)
KCC	Keyboard Common Contact
K-CODE	Extended Mercury Autocode (KDF9)
KC/S	Kilocycles per Second
KDR	Keyboard Data Recorder
KHZ	Kilohertz
KIEV	Russian Digital Computer
KIPO	Keyboard Input Printout
KIS	Keyboard Input Simulation
KISS	Automatic Coding System
KK	1,000,000
KL	Key Length
KLS	Knotted List Structure
KO.6	Programming Language similar to ALGOL
KOMPILER	Algebraic Compiler

KP	Key Pulsing
KP	Key Punch
KRYSTALL	Special Purpose Russian Computer
KS	Automatic Coding System
KSR	Keyboard Send-Receive
KV	Kilovolt
KW	Kilowatt
KWHR	Kilowatt Hour
KWIC	Key Word In Context
KWIT	Key Word In Title
KWOC	Key Word Out of Context
KY	Keying Device

L

L	Left
L	Level
L	Line
L	Load
L	Low
L1	Automatic Coding System
L2	Automatic Coding System
L6	Laboratories' Low-Level Linked List Language (Bell Telephone Laboratories)
LACONIQ	Laboratory Computer On-Line Inquiry Monitor
LAD	Logical Aptitude Device
LAFFF	Language to Aid Financial Fact Finders
LAG	Load and Go Assembler
LAM	Loop Adder and Modifier (Foxboro)
LANG	Language
LAP	Lesson Assembly Program
LAP	List Assembly Program
LAP	List Processing Language
LARC	Livermore Atomic Research Computer (UNIVAC)
LASER	Light Amplification by Simulated Emission of Radiation
LASL	Los Alamos Scientific Laboratory

LAT	Latitude
LB	Line Buffer
LBL	Label
LBT	Low Bit Test
LC	Last Card
LC	Library of Congress Classification
LC	Line Connector
LC	Line of Communications
LC	Lower Case
LCL	Linkage Control Language
LCM	Large Core Memory
LCP	Language Conversion Program
LCS	Large Core Storage
LD	Linear Decision
LD	Liquidated Damages
LD	Load
LD	Long Distance
LDA	Locate Drum Address
LDC	Latitude Data Computer
LDDS	Low Density Data System
LDE	Linear Differential Equation
LDP	Language Data Processing
LDR	Low Data Rate
LDRI	Low Data Rate Input
LDS	Large Disk Storage
LDT	Logic Design Translator
LDT	Long Distance Transmission

LDX	Long Distance Xerography
LE	Leading Edge
LE	Less than or Equal to (FORTRAN)
LEADS	Law Enforcement Automated Data System
LEAF	LISP Extended Algebraic Facility
LEAP	Language for the Expression of Associative Procedures
LEAR	Lockheed Electronics Assembly Program (MAC 16)
LEAR	Logistics Evaluation and Review Technique
LEASE	Lease Electronic Accounting System
LECOM	Compiler Language Similar to COMIT
LEO	Leo Computers Ltd. (British computer manufacturer)
LEO	Lyon's Electronic Office
LESS	Least Cost Estimating and Scheduling System (IBM)
LF	Line Feed
LF	Line Finder
LF	Logical File
LF	Low Frequency
LFE	Laboratory for Electronics
LG	Line Generator
LGP	Librascope General Purpose
LH	Left Hand
LI	Letter of Intent

LIBR	Library
LIFO	Last In-First Out
LIFT	Logically Integrated FORTRAN Translator (UNIVAC)
LIM	Limit
LIMAC	Large Integrated Monolithic Array Computer
LINC	Laboratory Instrument Computer (DEC)
LIOCS	Logical Input/Output Control System
LIPL	Linear Information Processing Language
LIS	Link Information Sciences
LISP	List Processing (language)
LISP	List Processor
LISP 1.5	List Processing 1.5
LISP A	LISP-like Programming System
LISPER	Limited Speech Recognition
LIST	List Processing Systems
LIT	Literal
LITE	Legal Information Through Electronics (USAF)
LIZARDS	Library Information Search and Retrieval Data System
L/L	Latitude/Longitude
LL	Lincoln Laboratory
LL	Low Level
LL	Lower Limit

LLLLLL	Laboratories Low-Level Linked List Language (Bell Telephone—pronounced L-six)
LLS	Long Left Shift
L/M	Lines per Minute
LOCAL	Laboratory Program for Computer-Assisted Learning
LOCI	Logarithmic Computing Instrument
LOCS	Librascope Operations Control System
LOCS	Logic and Control Simulator (IBM)
LOG	Logarithm
LOGALGOL	Logical Algorithmic Language
LOGEL	Logic Generating Language
LOGIPAC	Logical Processor and Computer
LOGLAN	Logical Language (University of Florida)
LOGO	Programming Language designed for elementary school children
LOGRAM	Logical Program
LOGTAB	Logic Tables
LOLITA	Language for the On-Line Investigation and Transformation of Abstractions
LOMA	Life Office Management Association
LOMUSS	Lockheed Multiprocessor Simulation System
LONG	Longitude

LORPGAC	Long Range Proving Ground Automatic Computer
LOS	Loss Of Signal
LOTIS	Logic, Timing, Sequencing (programming language)
LP	Line Printer
LP	Linear Programming
LP	List Processing
LP	List Processor
LP	Load Point
LP	Local Procurement
LPD	Didactic Programming Language
LPD	Language Processing and Debugging
LPG	Language de Programmation et de Gestion (CII)
LPL	Linear Programming Language
LPL	List Processing Language
LPM	Lines Per Minute
L-R	Left to Right
LRLTRAN	Lawrence Radiation Laboratory Translator
LRM	Limited Register Machine
LRS	Linguistic Research System (Univ. of Texas)
LRS	Long Right Shift
LS	Language Specification
LS	Least Significant
LS	Left Shift

LS	Low Speed
LSB	Least Significant Bit
LSC	LARC Scientific Compiler
LSC	Least Significant Character
LSD	Least Significant Digit
LSD	Low Speed Data
LSDL	Language for Systems Development
LSI	Large Scale Integration
LSP	Low Speed Printer
LST	Last
LT	Language Translation
LT	Less Than (FORTRAN)
LT	Logic Theory
LT-2	Automatic Coding System
LTD.	Limited
LTL	Literal
LTLA	Life Insurance Logistics Automated (HIS)
LTPL	Long Term Procedural Language
LUCH	Special Purpose Russian Computer
LUCID	Programming Language
LV	Low Voltage
LVL	Level
LYAPAS	Programming Language for Russian Computers
LYRIC	CAI Programming Language

M

M	Magnetic
M	Medium
M	Mega
M	Meter
M	Milli
M	Monitor
MA	Machine Accountant
MA	Mathematical Association (Great Britain)
MA	Memory Address
MA	Mercury-Atlas
MA	Message Assembler
MA	Milliampere
MA	Modify Address
MAA	Mathematical Association of America
MAC	Autocoding for the Ferranti Mercury Computer (Ferranti Mercury)
MAC	Machine Aided Cognition (Project MAC at M.I.T.)
MAC	Multiple Access Computer
MAC	Multiple Application Computer (Lockheed Electronics Co.)
MAC-360	Numerical Problem Solving Language (IBM System/360)
MACC	Modular Alter and Compose Console
MACE	Management Applications in a Computer Environment

MACH	Machine
MACMIS	Maintenance and Construction Management Information System
MACON	Matrix Connector Punched-card Programmer
MAD	Master Accession Document
MAD	Michigan Algorithm Decoder (programming language)
MAD	Multi-Aperature Device
MAD	Multiple Access Device
MAD	Multiply and Add
MADA	Multiple-Access Discrete-Address
MADAM	General Purpose Computer (built by Manchester University and Ferranti)
MADAM	Moderately Advanced Data Management
MADAM	Multi-purpose Automatic Data Analysis Machine
MADAM	Programming Language
MADAR	Malfunction Analysis Detection And Recording
MADBLOC	MAD Language Block Oriented Compiler (University of Colorado)
MADBUG	MAD Debugging System
MADCAP	Algebraic Translator
MADDAM	Macro-Module and Digital Differential Analyzer Machine(Burroughs Corp.)
MADDIDA	Magnetic Drum Digital Differential Analyzer
MADE	Microalloy Diffused Electrode

MADE	Minimum Airborne Digital Equipment
MADE	Multichannel Analog-to-Digital Data Encoder
MADM	Manchester Automatic Digital Machine (Manchester University)
MADRE	Magnetic Drum Receiving Equipment
MADT	Microalloy Diffused Base Transistor
MADTRAN	M.I.T. FORTRAN
MAECON	Mid-America Electronics Conference
MAG	Magnetic
MAGIC	Machine for Automatic Graphics Interface to a Computer (Dept. of Commerce)
MAGIC	Matrix Algebra General Interpretive Coding
MAGIC	Michigan Automatic General Integrated Computation
MAGIC	MIDAC Automatic General Integrated Computation
MAGIC-I	MIDAC Automatic General Integrated Computation
MAGLOC	Magnetic Logic Computer
MAGNACARD	Magnacard System (Magnavox Co.)
MAGNET	Programming Language
MAGNUS	Magnetic Tape Handling System
MAGPAP	Magic Paper
MAGPIE	Machine Automatic Generation of Paper Instead of Engines
MAID	MONROBOT Automatic Internal Diagnosis

MAINT	Maintenance
MAL	Macro Assembly Language
MAM	Multiple Access to Memory
MAMI	Machine-Aided Manufacturing Information
MAMOS	Monitor System
MANDATE	Management Data Engineering for Business and Industry
MANIAC	Mathematical Analyzer Numerical Integrator and Computer
MANIAC	Mechanical and Numerical Integrator and Computer
MANIP	Manual Input
MAP	Macro Assembly Program
MAP	Mathematical Analysis without Programming (M.I.T. system)
MAP	Matrix Algebra Interpretive Program
MAP	Model And Program
MAP	Multiple Allocation Procedure
MAPCHE	Mobile Automatic Programmed Checkout Equipment
MAPID	Machine Aided Program for Preparation of Instruction Data
MAPS	Multicolor Automatic Projection System (Litton)
MAR	Memory Address Register
MARC	Machine Readable Cataloging (Library of Congress)
MARGEN	Management Report Generator
MARI	Interpretive Program for Matrix Algebra

MARIS	Maritime Research Information Service
MARK I	Automatic Sequence Controlled Calculator
MARLIS	Multi-Aspect Relevance Linkage Information System
MARS	Machine Retrieval System
MARS	Management Analysis Reporting Service
MARS	Multiple Apertured Reluctance Switch (IBM)
MART	Maintenance Analysis Review Technique
MAS	Management Advisory Services
MASCOT	Motorola Automatic Sequential Computer Operated Tester (Motorola Corp.)
MASS	Monitor and Assembly System
MASS	Multiple Access Sequential Selection
MASTER	Matching Available Student Time to Educational Resources
MASTER	Microwave Amplification by the Simulated Emission of Radiation
MASTER	Multiple Access Shared Time Executive Routine
MATH	Mathematics
MATHLAB	On-line Programming System
MATH-MATIC	Programming System (UNIVAC I and II)
MATHPAC	Scientific/engineering Routine
MATIC	Multiple Area Technical Information Center

MATLAN	Matrix Language
MATPS	Machine Aided Technical Processing System
MATSUSHIA	Matsushia Communication Industrial Corporation (Japanese computer manufacturer)
MAUDE	Morse Automatic Decoder
MAVIN	Machine Assisted Vendor Information Network
MAX	Maximum
MAYBE	Compiler Language
MB	Memory Buffer
MBPS	Megabits Per Second
MBR	Memory Buffer Register
MC	Magnetic Core
MC	Manual Control
MC	Marginal Checking
MC	Master Control
MC	Megacycle
MC	Military Computer
M & C	Monitor and Control
MCBF	Mean Cycles Between Failures
MCC	Main Communications Center
MCC	Management Control Center
MCC	Multiple Computer Complex
MCCU	Multiple Communication Control Unit
MCG	Man-Computer Graphics
MCLR	Master Clear

MCM	Magnetic Core Memory
MCM	Monte Carlo Method
MCMJ	*Michigan Mathematical Journal*
MCOM	Mathematics of Computation
MCP	Master Control Program
MCP	Memory Centered Processor
MCP	Multichannel Communications Program
MCR	Magnetic Character Reader
MCR	Magnetic Character Recognition
MCR	Master Control Routine
MCS	Macrominiature High-Speed Computer System (Elliott Automation)
MCS	Master Control System
MCS	Medical Computer Services
MCS	Megacycles per Second
MCS	Multi-programmed Computer System
MCUG	Military Computers Users Group
MCW	Modulated Continuous Wave
MCX	Minimum Cost Estimating
MD	Magnetic Disk
MD	Magnetic Drum
MD	Main Drum
MD	Manual Data
MD	Message Data
MD	Messages per Day
MD	Monitor Displays
MDAC	Multiplying Digital-to-Analog Converter

MDE	Magnetic Decision Element
MDF	Main Distributing Frame
MDL	Macro Description Language
MDR	Memory Data Register
MDS	Memory Disk System
MDS	Modern Data Systems
MDT	Mean Down Time
MDTA	Man-power Development and Training Act
ME	Mechanical Efficiency
MEC	Mitsubishi Electric Corp. (Japanese computer manufacturer)
MEDAC	Medical Accounting Process
MEDLARS	Medical Literature Analysis and Retrieval System
MEDS	Medical Evaluation Data System
MEG	Megohm
MEGA	Million
MEM	Memory
MENTOR	Computer Assisted Instruction Programming Language
MERLIN	Digital Computer (Brookhaven National Laboratory)
MESM	Russian Digital Computer
MESY	Compiler Language similar to ALGOL
META 5	Syntax-directed Compiling Language
METAPLAN	META Programming Language
META-SYMBOL	Symbolic Processor
MF	Medium Frequency

MF	Microfiche
MFCM	Multi-Function Card Machine
MFD	Microfarad
MFG	Manufacturing
MFS	Magnetic Tape Field Search
MFT	Multiprogramming Fixed Tasks
MGC	Missile Guidance Computer
MGL	Matrix Generator Language
MGMT	Management
MGR	Manager
MH	Magnetic Head
MHz	Megahurtz
MI	Manual Input
MIACS	Manufacturing Information and Control System
MIB	Manual Input Buffer
MIC	Michigan Instructional Computer
MICA	Macro Instruction Compiler Assembler
MICR	Magnetic Ink Character Recognition
MICROMIN	Microminiature
MICRO-PAC	Micromodule Data Processor and Computer
MICS	Management Information and Control System
MI/DAC	Management Information/Decision and Control
MIDAC	Michigan Digital Automatic Computer (University of Michigan)

MIDAS	Modified Integration Digital/Analog Simulator
MIFACS	Medical Institutions Financial Accounting System
MILECON	Military Electronics Convention
MILITRAN	Simulation Programming Language
MILLI	One-thousandth
MILL. S.	Millisecond
MIL STD	Military Standard
MIMIC	Linguistic Compiler for Grammar Structure Work (Rand Corp.)
MIMO	Man In—Machine Out
MIN	Minimum
MIN	Minute
MINAC	Miniature Navigation Airborne Computer
MINI-TOK	Programming Language
MINSK-I	Russian Digital Computer (Moscow University)
MINSK-II	Russian Digital Computer (Moscow University)
MIOP	Multiplexing Input/Output Processors
MIP	Manual Input Processing
MIP	Manual Input Program
MIP	Matrix Inversion Program
MIP	Methods Improvement Program (IBM)
MIPE	Modular Information Processing Equipment

MIPS	Million Instructions Per Second
MIPS	Missile Impact Predictor Set
MIR	Memory Information Register
MIR	Memory Input Register
MIRACL	Management Information Report Access without Computer Languages
MIRFAC	Mathematics In Recognizable Form Automatically Compiled
MIRS	Manpower Information Retrieval System
MIS	Management Information System
MIS	Manufacturing Information System
MIS	Marketing Information System
MISC	Miscellaneous
MISHAP	Automatic Coding System
MISP	Medical Information System Programs
MISSIL	Management Information System Symbolic Interpretive Language
MISTIC	Michigan State Digital Computer (Michigan State University)
M.I.T.	Massachusetts Institute of Technology
MIT	Master Instruction Tape
MITILAC	Automatic Coding System
MITOL	Machine-Independent Telemetry-Oriented Language
MITSUBISHI	Mitsubishi Electric Corporation (Japanese computer manufacturer)
MJS	Automatic Coding System
MK	Manual Clock

ML	Machine Language
ML-I	Manipulation Language I
MLP	Machine Language Program
MLPCB	Multilayer Printed Circuit Boards
MLS	Multi-Language System
MLY	Multiply
M/M	Maximum/Minimum
MM	Millimeter
MMF	Micromicrofarad
MMS	Mass Memory Store
MMT	Memory Tester
MN	Manual
MNEMBLER	Mnemonic Assembler (SEL computers)
MO	Manual Output
MO	Miscellaneous Operation
M&O	Maintenance and Operations
MOBIDAC	Mobile Data Acquisition System
MOBIDIC	Mobile Digital Computer (Sylvania)
MOBL	Macro Oriented Business Language
MOC	Master Operational Controller
MOC	Mission Operation Computer
MOD	Model
MOD	Modular
MOD	Module
MODAC	Mountain Systems Digital Automatic Computer
MODEM	Modulator-Demodulator

MOL	Machine Oriented Language
MOLECOM	Molecularized Digital Computer
MON	Monitor
MONROBOT	Digital Computer (Monroe)
MONTECODE	Simulation Programming Language
MOP	Multiple On-line Programming
MOS	Management Operating System (IBM)
MOS	Manufacturing Operating System
MOS	Master Operating System
MOS	Metallic Oxide Semiconductor
MOS	Modular Operating System
MOSAIC	Macro Operation Symbolic Assembler and Information Compiler
MOSAIC	Ministry of Supply Automatic Integrator and Computer
MOWASP	Mechanization of Warehousing and Shipment Processing
MP	Main Program
MP	Multi-Processor
MPACS	Management Planning and Control System
MPPL	Multi-Purpose Processing Language
MPS	Mathematical Programming System
MPS	Multi-Programming System
MPSRG	Mathematical Programming System/360 Report Generator (IBM)
MPX	Multiprogramming Executive (IBM 1800)
MQ	Multiplier Quotient

MR	Memory Reference
MR	Memory Register
MRAD	Mass Random Access Disk
MRADS	Mass Random Access Data Storage
MRU	Machine Records Unit
MRWC	Multiple Read-Write Compute
MS	Macromodular System
MS	Magnetic Storage
MS	Management Science
MS	Mark Sense
MS	Mean Square
MS	Memory System
MS	Military Specification
MS	Military Standard
MS	Millisecond; one-thousandth of a second
MS	Most Significant
MSAC	Moore School Automatic Computer (University of Pennsylvania)
MSB	Most Significant Bit
MSC	Macro Selection Compiler
MSC	Most Significant Character
MSD	Most Significant Digit
MSEC	Millisecond
MSG	Message
MSI	Medium Scale Integration
MS/I	Multi-programming System/I (IBM)
MSIO	Mass Storage Input-Output

MSOS	Mass Storage Operating System
MSR	Mass Storage Resident
MSS	Management Science Systems
MSS	Mass Storage System
MST	Monolithic Systems Technology
MT	Machine Translation
MT	Magnetic Tape
MT	Maintenance Technician
MT	Mechanical Translation
MT	Multiple Transfer
MTAC	Mathematical Tables and Other Aids to Computation
MTBF	Mean Time Between Failures
MTC	Master Tape Control
MTC	Memory Test Computer
MTCF	Mean Time to Catastrophic Failure
MTCU	Magnetic Tape Control Unit
MTDS	Manufacturing Test Data System (IBM)
MTDS	Marine Tactical Data System
MTPF	Minimal Total Processing Time
MTPS	Magnetic Tape Programming System
MTR	Magnetic Tape Recorder
MTR	Monitor
MTRE	Magnetic Tape Recorder End
MTRS	Magnetic Tape Recorder Start
MTS	Magnetic Tape Station
MTS	Magnetic Tape System

MTS	Michigan Terminal System
MTS	Michigan Time-Sharing
MT/SC	Magnetic Tape/Selectric Composer (IBM)
MT/ST	Magnetic Tape/Selectric Typewriter (IBM)
MTT	Magnetic Tape Terminal
MTT	Magnetic Tape Transport
MTTC	Magnetic Tape Transport Controller
MTTD	Mean Time To Diagnosis
MTTF	Mean Time To Failure
MTTR	Mean Time To Repair
MTTR	Mean Time To Restore
MTU	Magnetic Tape Unit
MTU	Multiplexer and Terminal Unit
MTVAL	Master Tape Validation
MU	Machine Unit
MUL	Multiply
MULTICS	Multiplexed Information and Computing Service
MULTIPLE	Multipurpose Program that Learns
MUMPS	MGH Utility Multi-Programming System
MUPS	Multiple Utility Peripheral System
MURG	Machine Utilization Report Generator
MUX	Multiplex
MV	Mean Value
MV	Measured Value

MV	Millivolt
MVT	Multiprogramming with a Variable Number of Tasks (IBM)
MWI	Message Waiting Indicator
MX	Matrix
MX	Multiplex
MYRIAD	Digital Computer (designed and developed by Marconi Co. of England)
MYSTIC	Air Force Missile Test Center Automatic Coder

N

N	Nano
N	No
NA	Not Applicable
NA	Not Assigned
NA	Not Available
N/A	Numerical Analysis
NAA	National Association of Accountants
NABAC	Association for Bank Audit, Control, and Operation
NABUR	Naval Research Electronic Computer
NACAA	National Association of Computer Assisted Analysts
NACC	National Automatic Controls Conference
NACT	NCR Automatic Controller for Testing
NADGE	NATO Air Defense Ground Environment System
NAECON	National Aerospace Electronics Conference
NAEDS	National Association of Educational Data Systems
NANWEP	Navy Numerical Weather Prediction (CDC)
NAP	North American Philips
NAPE	National Association of Power Engineers

NAPM	National Association of Purchasing Management
NAPS	National Auxiliary Publications Service
NAPS	Nimbus Automatic Programming System
NAPSS	Numerical Analysis Problem Solving System
NAREC	Naval Research Electronic Computer
NARM	National Association of Relay Manufacturers
NAS	National Academy of Science
NASA	National Aeronautics and Space Administration
NASIS	National Association for State Information Systems
NASPA	National Society of Public Accountants
NATDC	Navy Airborne Tactical Data System
NATTS	National Association of Trade and Technical Schools
NAVA	National Audio Visual Association
NAVCOSSACT	Information Processing Systems
NB	No Bias
NBS	National Bureau of Standards
NC	No Change
NC	No Charge
NC	No Connection
NC	Non-Conformance

N/C	Numerical Control
NCA	Northwest Computing Association
NCC	National Computer Conference
NCC	National Computing Center
NCC	Norwegian Computing Center (Oslo, Norway)
NCI	National Computer Institute
NCI	National Computing Industries
NCI	Netherlands Centre for Informatics
NCI	Northeast Computer Institute
NCOS	Non-Concurrent Operating System (UNIVAC)
NCR	National Cash Register Company
NCS	National Computer Systems
NCS	Netherlands Computer Society
NCS	Numerical Control Society
NCTM	National Council of Teachers of Mathematics
ND	No Detect
NDRO	Nondestructive Readout
NDT	Nondestructive Testing
NE	Not Equal to (FORTRAN)
NEA	National Education Association
NEAC	Nippon Electric Automatic Computer
NEADAI	National Education Association Department of Audiovisual Instruction

NEAT	National Cash Register Electronic Autocoding Technique
NEAT	National Electronic Autocoding Technique (NCR)
NEBULA	Digital Computer (Oregon State University)
NEBULA	Natural Electronic Business User's Language (International Computers, Ltd.)
NEC	National Electric Code
NEC	National Electronics Conference
NEC	Nippon Electric Co. (Japanese computer manufacturer)
NECS	Nationwide Educational Computer Service
NEEDS	New England Educational Data Systems
NEG	Negative
NEIS	National Engineering Information System
NEL	Naval Electronics Laboratory
NELAT	Naval Electronics Laboratory Assembly Tester
NELIAC	Navy Electronics Laboratory International Algebraic Compiler
NEMA	National Electrical Manufacturers Association
NEREM	Northeast Electronics Research and Engineering Meeting
NETSET	Network Synthesis and Evaluation Technique

NF	Nanofarad
NFSR	National Foundation for Scientific Research (Belgium)
NG	New Generation
NI	Numerical Index
NIAM	Netherlands Institute for Audiovisual Media
NICAP	Assembly Language
NICB	National Industrial Conference Board
NICE	National Institute of Ceramic Engineers
NICE	NELIAC Implementers Council and Exchange
NICOL	Nineteen-Hundred/Commercial Language
NIDA	Numerically Integrated Differential Analyzer
NIDER	Netherlands Institute for Documentation and Filing
NIL	Nothing
NIP	NAREC Interpretive Programming System
NIPO	Negative Input - Positive Output
NIPPON	Nippon Electric Company (Japanese computer manufacturer)
NISARC	National Information Storage and Retrieval Centers
NJCC	National Joint Computer Committee (superseded by AFIPS)
NLR	Noise Load Ratio

NMA	National Management Association
NMA	National Microfilm Association
NMAA	National Machine Accountants Association (now DPMA)
NMCS	National Military Command System
NMCSSC	National Military Command System Support Center
NMEMBLER	Mnemonic Assembler
NMI	Nautical Miles
NMPS	Nautical Miles Per Second
NO	Number
NOC	Notice of Change
NOF	NCR Optical Font
NOL	Naval Ordnance Laboratory
NOM	Nominal
NOMA	National Office Management Association
NOMAD	Algebraic Compiler
NOMIS	Naval Ordnance Management Information System
NO-OP	No Operation
NOP	No Operation
N-OP	Non-Operational
NOR	Logical Operator
NORAD	North American Air Defense Command
NORC	Naval Ordnance Research Computer
NOSC	Naval Ordnance Systems Command

NOSY	Non-system (core saving operating system)
NOTS	Naval Ordnance Test Station
NOVA	Computer manufactured by DGC
NPEF	New Product Evaluation Form
NPL	National Physical Laboratory (England)
NPL	New Product Line
NPL	New Programmed Language (replaced by PL/1)
NPM	Counts Per Minute
NPS	Counts Per Second
NR	Not Required
NR	Number
NRC	National Research Council
NRECA	National Rural Electric Cooperative Association
NRM	Normalize
NRMA	National Retail Merchants Association
NRMG	Dutch Computer Society
NRTSC	Naval Reconnaissance and Technical Support Center
NRZ	Non-Return to Zero
NRZ1	Non-Return to Zero Change on One
NRZC	Non-Return to Zero Change
NRZL	Non-Return to Zero Level
NRZM	Non-Return to Zero Mark
NS	Nanosecond

NS	National Standard
NS	New System
NS	Next System
NS	Non-Standard
NS	Not Specified
NS	Number System
NSA	National Security Agency
NSA	Netherlands Society for Automation
NSC	National Simulation Council
NSEC	Nanosecond
NSEIP	Norwegian Society for Electronic Information Processing
NSF	National Science Foundation
NSI	Nonstandard Item
NSL	National Science Library
NSPA	National Society of Public Accountants
NSPE	National Society of Professional Engineers
NSPI	National Society for Programmed Instruction
NSTA	National Science Teachers Association
NT	No Transmission
NT	Not Tested
NTC	National Telemetering Conference
NTDC	Naval Training Device Center
NTDS	Naval Tactical Data System
NTG	Nachrichtentechnische Gesellschaft (German Communications Society)

NTIS	National Technical Information Service
NTS	Not To Scale
NUCOL	Numerical Control Programming Language (Italy)
NUCOM	Version of APT
NUL	Null
NUM	Number
NUM	Numerator
NUM	Numeric
NUMBERICORD	Machine Tool Director
N U SPEAK	List Processing Programming Language
NVAL	Not Available
NWDS	Number of Words
NYAP	New York Assembly Program
NYSE	New York Stock Exchange
NYSE-VAB	New York Stock Exchange Voice Answer Back

O

O	Octal
O	Output
OA	Operations Analysis
OA	Operations Analyst
OAO	Orbiting Astronomical Observatory
OARAC	Office of Air Research Automatic Computer
OASIS	Programming Language
OASYS	Order Allocation System
OB	Obsolete
O-B	Octal-to-Binary
OB	Output Buffer
OC	On Call
OC	Operating Characteristics
OC	Operational Computer
OCAL	On-Line Cryptanalytic Aid Language
OCAS	On-Line Cryptanalytic Aid System
OCL	Operators Control Language
OCR	Optical Character Reader
OCR	Optical Character Recognition
OCR-A	Optical Character Recognition-Font A
OCR-B	Optical Character Recognition-Font B
OCRUA	Optical Character Recognition Users Association
OCT	Octal
O-D	Octal-to-Decimal

OD	Output Data
OD	Outside Diameter
ODA	Operational Data Analysis
ODA	Operational Design and Analysis
ODG	Operational Design Group
ODP	Original Document Processing
ODRA	Polish Digital Computer
ODT	Octal Debugging Technique
ODU	Output Display Unit
OE	Office of Education
OECD	Organization for Economic Cooperation and Development
OEIC	Oki Electric Industry Company (Japanese computer manufacturer)
OEM	Original Equipment Manufacturers
OEMI	Office Equipment Manufacturers Institute
OEO	Office of Economic Opportunity
OFF	Office
O-H	Octal-to-Hexadecimal
OJT	On-the-Job Training
OKLAHOMA UNIV	Oklahoma University Computer
OKRA	Basic Autocoder Assembler (University of Oklahoma)
OL	On Line
O/L	On-Line
OL	Open Loop
OL	Overlap
OLC	On-Line Computer

OLERT	On-Line Executive for Real Time
OLHMIS	On-Line Hospital Management Information System
OLIS	Operating Systems Implementation Language (Burroughs Corp.)
OLM	On-Line Monitor
OLPARS	On-Line Pattern Analysis and Recognition System
OLPS	On-Line Programming System
OLRT	On Line—Real Time
OLSC	On-Line Scientific Computer
OLSS	On-Line Software System
OLTEP	On-Line Test Executive Program (IBM System/360)
OM	Operations Maintenance
OMAT	Office of Manpower Automation and Training (Labor Dept.)
OMIBAC	Ordinal Memory Inspecting Binary Automatic Computer
OMNICODE	Automatic Coding System
OMNIFAX	Automatic Coding System
OMNIFLEX	Integrated Service Routine
OMNITAB	Programming Language
OMPR	Optical Mark Page Reader
OMR	Optical Mark Reader
ONR	Office of Naval Research
OOL	Operator Oriented Language
OOPS	Off-line Operating Simulator
OP	Operation
OP	Output

OPER	Operator
OPERG	Operating
OPL-1	Open-Ended Programming System
OPM	Operations Per Minute
OPN	Open
OPP	Octal Print Punch
OPR	Optical Page Reader
OPS	On-line Process Synthesizer
OPS-3	On-line Simulation System
OPSCAN	Optical Scanning Users Group
OPT	Optical
OPTIMA	Linear Programming System (CDC 6000 Series)
OR	Logical Operator
O/R	On Request
OR	Operations Requirement
OR	Operations Research
OR	Optical Reader
ORACLE	Oak Ridge Automatic Computer and Logical Engine
ORBIT	On-line Retrieval of Bibliographic Data
ORBIT	ORACLE Binary Internal Translator
ORDVAC	Ordnance Variable Automatic Computer
ORG	Organization
ORIG	Origin
ORION	Time Shared Computer System (mfg. by Ferranti, Ltd.)

ORSA	Operations Research Society of America
ORT	Operational Readiness Test
OS	Odd Symmetric
OS	Operating System
OS-3	Time-sharing Operating System (Oregon State CDC 3300 system)
OS/360	Operating System IBM System/360
OSAS	Symbolic Coding System
OSD	Office of the Secretary of Defense
OSR	Optical Scanning Recognition
OSS	Programming Language for Russian Computers
OST	President's Office of Science and Technology
OT	Overtime
OTAC	Ordnance Tank Automotive Command
OTRAC	Oscillogram Trace Reader
OUT	Output
OUTRAN	Output Translator
OVFLO	Overflow
OVL	Overlap
OVLY	Overlay

P

P	Packed
P	Parity
P	Pico (10 to the minus twelfth power)
P	Plug
P	Punch
PA	Paper Advance
PA	Program Address
PA	Program Analysis
PA	Pulse Amplifier
PABX	Private Automatic Branch Exchange
PAC	Pedagogic Automatic Computer
PACC	Product Administration and Contract Control System (UNIVAC)
PACE	Packaged Cram Executive (NCR)
PACE	Performance And Cost Evaluation
PACE	Precision Analogue Computing Equipment
PACE	Programming Analysis Consulting Education
PACER	Program Assisted Console Evaluation and Review
PACER	Programmed Automatic Communications Equipment
PACT	Pay Actual Computer Time
PACT	Production Analysis Control Technique

PACT	Programmed Automatic Circuit Tester
PAI	Programmer Appraisal Instrument
PAL	Interactive Programming System
PAL	Pedagogic Algorithmic Language
PAL	Precision Artwork Language
PAL	Process Assembly Language (GE/PAC computers)
PAL	Programmed Application Library (IBM)
PAL	Symbolic Machine-Oriented Language
PALIS	Property and Liability Information System
PAM	Personnel Accounting Management
PAM	Pulse Amplitude Modulation
PAMS	Proceedings of the American Mathematical Society
PANON	String Processing Programming Language
PAR	Parameter
PAR	Program Appraisal and Review
PAR	Project Audit Report
PARD	Precision Annotated Retrieval Display
PAREX	Programmed Accounts Receivable Extra Service
PARS	Passenger Airlines Reservation System
PART	Parts Allocation Requirements Technique
PARTNER	Proof of Analog Results Through Numerically Equivalent Routine (Honeywell)

PASC	Pan American Standards Committee
PASCAL	Philips Automatic Sequence Calculator
PASS	Program Aid Software Systems
PASSIM	President's Advisory Staff on Scientific Information Management
PAT	Patent
PAT	Personalized Array Translator
PAT	Process and Tool Oriented Program
PAT	Programmer Aptitude Test
PAT	Programmer Aptitude Tester
PATN	Pattern
PATSY	Program Automatic Testing System (ICT)
PAX	Private Automatic Exchange
P/B	Piggy Back
PB	Plug Board
PB	Publications Bulletin
PB	Push Button
PBDG	Push Button Data Generator
P-BIT	Parity Bit
PBX	Private Branch Exchange
PC	Paper Change
PC	Printed Circuit
PC	Priority Control
PC	Process Control
PC	Program Coordination
PC	Program Counter
PC	Punched Card

PCAM	Punched Card Accounting Machinery
PCDC	Punched Card Data Processing
PCH	Punch
PCHG	Punching
PCM	Pulse Code Modulation
PCM	Punched Card Machine
PCMI	Photo Chronic Micro Image (NCR)
PCMS	Punched Card Machine System
PCOS	Primary Communications Oriented System
PCP	Parallel Cascade Processor (Foxboro)
PCP	Primary Control Program
PCP	Process Control Processor
PCP	Processor Control Program
PCP	Program Change Proposal
PCP	Punched Card Punch
PCR	Program Control Register
PCR	Punched Card Reader
PCS	Process Control System
PD	Per Diem
PD	Peripheral Device
PD	Program for Descriptor Query
PDA	Patient Data Automation
PDIS	Proceedings of the National Symposia
PDL	Procedure Definition Language
PDM	Pulse Duration Modulation
PDP	Programmed Data Processor

PDPS	Parts Data Processing System (Bell Telephone)
PDQ	Programmed Data Quantizer
PDR	Preliminary Design Review
PDR	Processed Data Recorder
PDR	Program Discrepancy Report
PDR	Program Document Requirement
PDS	Program Data Source
PE	Professional Engineer
PE	Project Engineer
PE	Purchased Equipment
PED	Personnel Equipment Data
PEER	Project Engineer Evaluation Report
PEM	Photoelectromagnetic
PENCIL	Pictorial Encoding Language
PENNCODE	Floating Point Interpretive Routine (PENNSTAC)
PENNSTAC	Penn State Automatic Computer (Pennsylvania State University)
PEP	Program Evaluation Procedure
PEPR	Precision Encoding and Pattern Recognition
PERCOS	Performance Coding System
PERGO	Project Evaluation and Review with Graphic Output
PERK	Performance Computer
PERT	Program Evaluation and Review Technique

PERT	Program Evaluation Research Task
PES	Photoelectric Scanner
PEST	Monitor Program (PHOENIX computer)
PET	Peripheral Equipment Tester
PEWTER	PERT Without Tears
PF	Page Footing
P/G	Programmer Group
PGEC	Professional Group on Electronic Computers
PGM	Program
PH	Page Heading
PHD	Parallel Head per Track Disk
PHENO	Precise Hybrid Elements for Nonlinear Operations
PHLAG	Phillips Petroleum Load and Go System
PHOENIX	Digital Computer (developed by Mitre Corp.)
PI	Parallel Input
PI	Performance Index
PI	π= 3.14159 26535 89793 23846 26433
PI	Priority Interrupt
PI	Program Indicator
PI	Program Instruction
PI	Program Interrupt
PI	Programmed Information
PI	Programmed Instruction

PI	Proprietary Information
PIA	Peripheral Interface Adapter
PIC	Program Interrupt Control
PICA	Power Industry Computer Applications Conference
PICA	Printing Industry Computer Associates
PICO	Airborne Computer (Honeywell)
PICOMM	Digital Computer (Potter Instrument Co.)
PICS	Personnel Information Communication System
PIE	Parallel Instruction Execution
PIE	Public Information Exchange
PILOT	Printing Industry Language for Operation of Typesetting
PIN	Police Information Network
PIN	Program Identification Number
PINT	Purdue Interpretive Programming and Operating System
PIOCS	Physical Input/Output Control System
PIOU	Parallel Input/Output Unit
PIP	Peripheral Interchange Program
PIP	Problem Input Preparation
PIP	Program In Progress
PIP	Project on Information Processing
PISW	Process Interrupt Status Word
PIT	Peripheral Input Tape

PIU	Plug-In Unit
PKD	Packed
PKMAD	Monitored Automatic Debugging System
PL	Production Language
PL	Programming Language
PL/1	Programming Language
PL360	Programming Language for the IBM System/360 Computer
PLACE	Programming Language for Automatic Checkout Equipment
PLAN	Problem Language Analyzer (IBM)
PLANIT	Programming Language for Interactive Teaching
PLANS	Program Logistics and Network Scheduling System
PLANT	Program for Linguistic Analysis of Natural Plants
PLATO	Programmed Logic for Automatic Teaching Operations
PLIANT	PL/1 Application Nucleus Tools
PLIANT	Procedural Language Implementing Analog Techniques (IBM)
PL/S	Programming Language for Systems
PLT	Program Library Tape
PLUS	PERT—Life Cycle Unified System (IBM)
PLUS	Program Library Update System
PLUS	Program Loading, Updating and Selection (Honeywell)
PM	Post Mortem

PM	Preventive Maintenance
PM	Procedures Manual
PMC	Program Marginal Checking
PMC	Pseudo Machine Code
PMR	Pacific Missile Range
PMS	Processor, Memories and Switches
PMS	Program Management System
PMS	Project Management System
P-N	Positive-Negative
PN	Project Number
PNC	Programmed Numerical Control
PNCH	Punch
PNDC	Parallel Network Digital Computer (IBM)
PNEC	Proceedings of the National Electronics Conference
PO	Parallel Output
PO	Purchase Order
POD	Point-of-Origin Device
POGO	Programmer Oriented Graphics Operation
POGODA	Special Purpose Russian Computer
POL	Problem Oriented Language
POL	Procedure Oriented Language
POL	Process Oriented Language
POLIZ	Interpreter for the SETUN Computer
POLYTRAN	Polytranslation Analysis and Programming
POM	Operations per Minute

POOL	Users Association (General Precision)
POP	Power On/Off Protection
POP	Programmed Operator
POP	Programmed Operators and Primitives
POP 2	Programming Language (Edinburgh University)
POPS	Pantograph Optical Projection System
POR	Problem Oriented Routine
POS	Point-of-Sale
POS	Positive
POS	Primary Operating System
POSE	Programming Language
POSEIDON	Digital Computer (mfg. by Ferranti Ltd.)
POTC	PERT Orientation and Training Center
POUCHE	Program Distribution Service of the AICHE
PP	Pages
PP	Peripheral Processor
PP	Preprocessor
PP	Print-Punch
PPA	Professional Programmers Association
PPE	Problem Program Efficiency
PPI	Plan Position Indicator
PPM	Pulse-Position Modulation
PPM	Pulses Per Minute
PPS	Pulses Per Second

PPT	Punched Paper Tape
PPU	Peripheral Processing Unit
PR	Pattern Recognition
PR	Periodic Report
PR	Print
PR	Procurement Regulation
PR	Program Register
PR	Program Requirement
PR	Purchase Request
PRD	Printer Dump
PRD	Program Requirements Document
PREC	Precision
PRELIM	Preliminary
PREP	Programmed Educational Package (UNIVAC)
PREP	Project Return Evaluation Program
PREPARE	Plan for Retraining of Employable Persons As Related to EDP
PRI	Primary
PRIME	Programmed Instruction for Management Education
PRINT	Pre-edited Interpretive System
PRISM	Programmed Integrated System Maintenancc
PRM	Primary
PROC	Procedure
PROC	Processor
PROC	Programming Computer
PROCOMP	Process Computer

PROCOMP	Program Compiler
PRODAC	Programmed Digital Automatic Control
PROF	Profession
PROF	Professional
PROF	Professor
PROFIT	Programmed Reviewing, Ordering, and Forecasting Inventory Technique (Honeywell)
PROG	Program
PROG	Programming
PROG ANAL	Programming Analyst
PROM	Programmable Read-Only Memory
PROMOCOM	Project Monitor and Control Method
PROMPT	Program Monitoring and Planning Techniques
PRONTO	Program for Numerical Tool Operation
PROP	Performance Review for Operating Programs
PROSA	Programming Language (Siemens computer)
PROSPRO	Process Supervisory Program (IBM 1800)
PROXI	Projection by Reflected Optics from Xerographic Images
PROXY	Simulator
PRS	Pattern Recognition Society
PRS	Pattern Recognition System
PRT	Portable Remote Terminal

PRT	Printer
PRT	Production Run Tape
PRTY	Priority
PSC	Peripheral Systems Corporation
PSEC	Picosecond; one-trillionth of a second
PSI	Pressure Sensitive Identification
PSI	Proto Synthex Indexing
PSP	Power System Planning (IBM)
PSS	Proprietary Software Systems
PSW	Program Status Word
PSYCO	Princeton Syntax Compiler
PT	Paper Tape
PT	Partially Tested
PT	Part Time
PT	Pencil Tube
PT	Performance Test
PT	Point
PT	Program Table
PT	Program Time
PT	Punched Tape
PTC	Programmed Transmission Control (IBM)
PTP	Paper Tape Punch
PTR	Paper Tape Reader
PTR	Printer
PTS	Program Test System
PTS	Pure Time-Sharing

PTT	Program Test Tape
PTT	Push To Talk
PU	Power Unit
PU	Processing Unit
PUDL	Push Down List
PUFFT	Purdue University Fast FORTRAN Translator
PUSAS	Proposed USA Standard
PW	Pulse Width

R

R	Read
R	Reader
R	Resistor
R	Reverse
R	Right
RACE	Random Access Computer Equipment
RACE	Random Access Control Equipment
RACE	Rapid Automatic Checkout Equipment
RACS	Remote Access Computing System
RACT	Remote Access Computer Technique
RAD	Radian
RAD	Random Access Data
RAD	Rapid Access Disk
RAD	Rapid Access Drive
RADAC	Rapid Automatic Digital Computing System
RADAS	Random Access Discrete Address
RADC	Rome Air Development Center
RADIR	Random Access Document Indexing and Retrieval
RAES	Remote Access Editing System
RAFT	RECOMP Algebraic Formula Translator
RAI	Random Access and Inquiry
RAID	Remote Access Interactive Debugger

Q

QA	Query Analyzer
QADS	Quality Assurance Data System
Q & D	Quick and Dirty
QED	Conversational Text Editor
QISAM	Queued Indexed Sequential Access Method
QIT	Quality Information and Test System
QL	Query Language
QR	Quick Response
QSAM	Queued Sequential Access Method
QT	Queueing Theory
QTAM	Queued Telecommunications Access Method
QTY	Quantity
QUAP	Questionnaire Analysis Program
QUEASY	Automatic Coding System
QUEST	Quality Electrical System Test
QUICK	Automatic Coding System
QUICK	Queens University Interpretive Coder, Kingston (Queen's University Computing Centre)
QUICKSCRIPT	Programming Language Similar to SIMSCRIPT
QUICKTRAN	On-Line version of FORTRAN (IBM computer)
QUIP	Query Interactive Processor
QUOT	Quotient

RAIR	Random Access Information Retrieval
RAM	Random Access Memory
RAMAC	Random Access Method of Accounting and Control (IBM)
RAMIS	Rapid Access Management Information System
RANDAM	Random Access Nondestructive Advanced Memory
RAP	Assembly Program (UNIVAC computer)
RAPPI	Random Access Plan Position Indicator
RAPS	Retrieval Analysis and Presentation System
RASTAC	Random Access Storage and Control
RASTAD	Random Access Storage and Display
RATE	Remote Automatic Telemetry Equipment
RAX	Remote Access Computing System (IBM)
RAYDAC	Raytheon Digital Automatic Computer
RAZDAN	Russian Digital Computer
RB	Return to Bias
RBP	Registered Business Programmer
RC	Remote Control
RCA	Radio Corporation of America
RCC	Remote Communications Complex
RCO	Remote Control Oscillator
RD	Read

R & D	Research and Development
RDC	Remote Data Collection
RDP	Radar Data Processing
RDR	Read Drum
RDT	Remote Data Transmitter
RDY	Ready
R & E	Research and Engineering
REAC	Reeves Electronic Analog Computer
REACT	Register Enforced Automated Control Technique
READ	Real-time Electronic Access and Display
READIX	General Purpose Computer
REALCOM	Real-time and Communications Computer
REAP	Remote Entry Acquisition Package
REC	Record
REC	Request for Engineering Change
RECIPE	RECOMP Computer Interspective Program Expeditor
RECOMP	General Purpose Computer
RECOMP	Recomplement
RECSYS	Recreation Systems Analysis
REDAP	Re-entrant Data Processing
REF	Reference
REG	Register
REGNM	Register Name
REL	Rapidly Extensible Language

REL	Release
RELSIM	On-Line Language for Discrete Simulation in Social Science Research
REM	Remainder
REMIS	Real Estate Management Information System
REMRAND	Remington Rand UNIVAC (now UNIVAC Division of Sperry Rand Corp.)
REPAC	General Purpose Computer
REPRO	Reproducer
REQ	Request
RES	Research
RESETRON	Reservations by Electronics (Western Airlines)
RESISTORS	Radically Emphatic Students Interested in Science, Technology, Or Research Studies
RETAIN	Remote Technical Assistance and Information Network
RETMA	Radio-Electronics-Television Manufacturers Association (name changed to EIA)
REW	Rewind
REX	Real-Time Executive (UNIVAC)
RF	Read Forward
RF	Report Footing
RFI	Radio Frequency Interference
RFI	Request For Information
RFL	Report/File Language

RFMS	Remote File Management System
RFP	Request For Proposal
RFQ	Request For Quotation
RGL	Report Generator Language
R/GPSS	Remote/General Purpose Simulation System
RH	Report Heading
RH	Right Hand
RI	Read In
RICE UNIVERSITY	Rice University Computer
RIMM	Research Institute for Mathematical Machines (Czechoslovakia)
RITE	Rapidata Interactive Text Editor
RJE	Remote Job Entry
RKW	Foundation for Automation of German Industry (West Germany)
R-L	Right to Left
RLP	Data Reduction Language
RM	Record Mark
RMC	Rod Memory Computer (NCR)
RN	Random Number
RO	Read-Out
RO	Receive Only
ROAR	Royal Optimizing Assembly Routine
ROBIN	Remote On-Line Business Information Network
ROCAPPI	Research on Computer Applications in the Printing and Publishing Industries

ROCR	Remote Optical Character Recognition
ROM	Read-Only Memory
ROPP	Receive-Only Page Printer
ROS	Read-Only Storage
ROS	Resident Operating System
ROTR	Receive-Only Typing Reperforator
RP	Report
RPC	Royal Precision Computer
RPG	Report Program Generator
RPL	Radar Processing Language
RPL	Running Program Language
RPM	Reliability Performance Measure
RPM	Revolutions Per Minute
RPQ	Request for Price Quotation
RPQ	Request for Product Quotation
RPR	Read Printer
RPRT	Report
RPS	Remote Processing Service
RPS	Revolutions Per Second
RPS	Rotational Position Sensing
RPSM	Resources Planning and Scheduling Method
RPT	Report
RQS	Rate Quoting System
R/R	Record-Retransmit
RR	Register to Register Instruction
RR	Remove and Replace

RR	Repetition Rate
RR	Round Robin
RRU	Remington Rand UNIVAC (now UNIVAC Division of Sperry Rand Corp.)
RS	Remote Station
RS	Reset Key
RS	Right Shift
R & S	Research and Statistics
RSDP	Remove Site Data Processor
RSM	Resource Management System
RSMPS	Romanian Society for Mathematics and Physical Sciences
RSP	Record Select Program
RSVP	Report Preparation and Information Retrieval Language
RT	Real-Time
RT	Remote Terminal
RT	Reperforator/Transmitter
RTB	Read Tape Binary
RTC	Real-Time Command
RTC	Real-Time Computer
RTCC	Real-Time Computer Complex
RTCF	Real-Time Computer Facility
RTCS	Real-Time Computer System
RTCU	Real-Time Control Unit
RTD	Read Tape Decimal
RTD	Real-Time Display
RTDC	Real-Time Data Channel

RTDHS	Real-Time Data Handling System
RT/IOC	Real-Time Input/Output Controller
RTIRS	Real-Time Information Retrieval System
RTL	Real-Time Language
RTM	Real-Time Monitor
RTMOS	Real-Time Multiprogramming Operating System (GE/PAC computers)
RTOS	Real-Time Operating System
RTS	Radar Tracking Station
RTS	Reactive Terminal Service
RTSS	Real-Time Scientific System
RTTY	Radio Teletypewriter Communications
RTU	Remote Terminal Unit
RTX	Real-Time Executive
RUG	RECOMP Users Group
RUSH	Remote Use of Shared Hardware
RW	Read-Write
R/W	Read-Write
RWC	Read, Write, Compute
RWD	Rewind Tape
RX	Register to Indexed Storage Instruction
RZ	Return to Zero
RZL	Return to Zero Level
RZM	Return to Zero Mark

S

S	Second
S	Sign
S	Switch
SA	Semi-Automatic
SA	Symbolic Assembler
SAAB	Svenska Aeroplan AB (Swedish computer manufacturer)
SAB	System Advisory Board
SABE	Society for Automating Better Education
SABE	Society for Automation in Business Education
SABRAC	Sabra Computer
SABRE	Sales and Business Reservations Done Electronically (American Airlines)
SAC	Assembly Routine
SAC	Semi-Automatic Coding
SAC	Strategic Air Command
SACCS	Strategic Air Command Control System
SADAP	Simplified Automatic Data Plotter
SADC	Sequential Analog-Digital Computer
SADIC	Solid-State Analog-to-Digital Computer
SADIE	Scanning Analog-to-Digital Input Equipment

SADSAC	Sampled Data Simulator and Computer
SADSAC	Seiler Algol Digitally Simulated Analog Computer
SAE	Society of Automative Engineers, Inc.
SAEH	Society for Automation in English and the Humanities
SAFA	Society for the Fine Arts
SAGE	Semi-Automatic Ground Environment Computer
SAHYB	Simulation of Analog and Hybrid Computers
SAIL	Automatic Coding System
SAINT	Symbolic Automatic Integrator
SAKI	Self-organizing Automatic Keyboard Instructor
SAL	Symbolic Assembly Language
SAL	Systems Assembly Language
SALE	Simple Algebraic Language for Engineers
SALEM	Programming Language for Expressing Solutions of Partial Differential Equations
SALT	Assembly Language (UNIVAC III)
SAM	Selective Auto Monitoring Tracing Routine
SAM	Sequential Access Method
SAM	Society for Advancement of Management
SAM	Sort And Merge

SAM	System Activity Monitor
SAME	Society of American Military Engineers
SAMIS	Structural Analysis and Matrix Interpretive System
SAMPE	Society of Aerospace Material and Process Engineers
SAMS	Satellite Automonitor System
SAP	Share Assembly Program
SAP	Symbolic Address Program
SAP	Systems Assurance Program
SAPE	Society for Professional Education
SAPIENT	Symbolic Assembly Program
SAPO	Czechoslovakian Digital Computer
SASM	Society for Science and Mathematics
SASS	Society for the Social Sciences
SATIN	SAGE Air Traffic Integration
SATIRE	Semi-Automatic Technical Information Retrieval
SAVE	Society of American Value Engineers
SAVITAR	Sanders Associates Video Input/Output Terminal Access Resource
SB	Serial Binary
SB	Service Bureau
SB	Straight Binary
SBC	Service Bureau Corporation (Subsidiary of IBM)
SBM	System Balance Measure

SBUG	Service Bureau Users Group (NCR)
SC	Simulation Council
S-C	Stromberg-Carlson
SCADA	Supervisory Control and Data Acquisition
SCADS	Simulation of Combined Analog Digital Systems (Carnegie Tech)
SCAMPS	Small Computer Analytical and Mathematical Programming System
SCAN	Stock Market Computer Answering Service
SCAN	Student Career Automated Network
SCAT	Share Compiler Assembler and Translator
SCDP	Society of Certified Data Processors
SCERT	Systems and Computers Evaluation and Review Technique
SCH	Schedule
SCI	Science
SCI	Simulation Councils, Inc.
SCM	Small Core Memory
SCMA	Systems Communications Management Association
SCOPAC	Optimizing FORTRAN-like Compiler
SCOPE	Operating System (CDC 6000 Series)
SCOPE	Sequential Customer Order Processing Electronically
SCOPE	Service Center of Private Enterprise
SCORE	COBOL Information Retrieval and Reporting System

SCORE	Satellite Computer Operated Readiness Equipment
SCORE	Selection Copy and Reporting System
SCP	Symbolic Conversion Program
SCR	Scratch
SCRIBE	Scoring and Data Transcription Computer
SCRIPT	Scientific and Commercial Subroutine Interpreter and Program Translator
SCS	Society for Computer Simulation
SCS	Southern Computer Service
SCS	Supervisory Control System
SCUP	School Computer Use Plan (CDC)
SDA	Source Data Acquisition
SDA	Source Data Automation
SDAP	Systems Development Analysis Program
SDAS	Scientific Data Automation System
SDC	Scientific Documentation Centre (Rumania)
SDC	Stabilization Data Computer (Burroughs Corp.)
SDCC	San Diego Computing Center
SDE	Society of Data Educators
SDE	Students for Data Education
SDI	Selective Dissemination of Information
SDI	Source Data Information
SDLC	Synchronous Data Link Control

SDP	Supreme Data Processing (England)
SDPA	Swedish Data Processing Association
SDR	System Design Review
SDS	Simulating Digital Systems
SDS	System Design Specification
SE	Standard Error
SE	Systems Engineer
SE	Systems Engineering
SEA	Société d'Éléctronique et d'Automatisme (French computer manufacturer)
SEA	Society of Electronics and Automation (France)
SEAC	Standards Eastern Automatic Computer (NBC)
SEAL	Standard Electronic Accounting Language
SEC	Secant
SEC	Second
SEC	Simple Electronic Computer
SECH	Hyperbolic Secant
SECO	Sequential Coding
SECT	Section
SECTAM	Southern Conference on Theoretical and Applied Mechanics
SEDIT	Sophisticated String Editor
SEDS	Society for Educational Data Systems
SEEK	Systems Evaluation and Exchange of Knowledge

SEESAW	Automatic Coding System
SEG	Segment
SEL	Select
SEL	Standard Elektrik Lorenz AG (German computer manufacturer)
SEL	Systems Engineering Laboratories, Inc.
SEMA	Société d'Économie et de Mathematique Appliqués (French programming organization)
SEN	Sense
SENTOS	Sentinel Operating System
SEP	Scientific and Engineering Personnel
SEP	Standard Electronic Package
SEPOL	Settlement Problem-Oriented Language
SEPOL	Soil Engineering Problem-Oriented Language
SEQ	Sequence
SER	Serial
SEREL	Société d'Éxploitation et de Récherches Éléctroniques (French computer manufacturer)
SERV	Service
SESOME	Service, Sort and Merge
SET	Self-Extending Translator
SETAR	Serial Event Time and Recorder
SETI	European Society for the Processing of Information
SETUN	Russian Digital Computer

SF	Shift Forward
SF	Standard Form
S/F	Store and Forward
SFAC	Swiss Federation of Automatic Control
SFD-ALGOL	System Function Description—ALGOL
SFF	Straight Fixed Fee
SGL	Signal
SGSR	Society for General Systems Research
SH	Shift
SHA	Software Houses Association (Great Britain)
SHADOW	String Manipulating Programming Language
SHARE	Computer Users Group (IBM Computers)
SHARE	Society to Help Avoid Redundant Effort
SHAS	Shared Hospital Accounting System (IBM)
SHF	Superhigh Frequency
SHOAP	Symbolic Horribly Optimizing Assembly Program (Case Institute of Technology)
SHORTCODE	Univac Short Code
SI	Storage Immediate
SIAM	Society for Industrial and Applied Mathematics
SIBC	Snake-In-the-Box Code

SIC	Semiconductor Integrated Circuits
SIC	Special Interest Committee (ACM)
SICEJ	Society of Instrument and Control Engineers of Japan
SICOM	Interpretive System (Control Data computer)
SICOM	Securities Industry Communications
SID	Society for Information Display
SIEMENS	West German Electronics Company and computer manufacturer
SIFOR	Simulation Language
SIFT	Share Internal FORTRAN Translator
SIG	Signal
SIG	Special Interest Group
SIGACT	Special Interest Group on Automata and Computability Theory (ACM)
SIG/AH	Special Interest Group Arts and Humanities (ASIS)
SIG/ALP	Special Interest Group Automate & Language Processing (ASIS)
SIGART	Special Interest Group on Artificial Intelligence (ACM)
SIG/BC	Special Interest Group Biomedical and Chemical Information Systems (ASIS)
SIGBDP	Special Interest Group on Business Data Processing (ACM)
SIGBIO	Special Interest Group on Biomedical Computing (ACM)
SIG/BSS	Special Interest Group Behavioral and Social Sciences (ASIS)

SIGCAS	Special Interest Group on Computers and Society (ACM)
SIG/CBE	Special Interest Group on Costs, Budgeting, and Economics (ASIS)
SIGCOMM	Special Interest Group on Data Communications (ACM)
SIGCOSIM	Special Interest Group on Computer Systems Installation Management (ACM)
SIGCPR	Special Interest Group on Computer Personnel Research (ACM)
SIG/CR	Special Interest Group Classification Research (ASIS)
SIGCSE	Special Interest Group on Computer Science Education (ACM)
SIGCUE	Special Interest Group on Computer Users in Education (ACM)
SIGDA	Special Interest Group on Design Automation (ACM)
SIG/ES	Special Interest Group Education for Information Science (ASIS)
SIGFIDET	Special Interest Group on File Description and Translation (ACM)
SIG/FIS	Special Interest Group on Foundations of Information Science (ASIS)
SIGGRAPH	Special Interest Group for Graphical Display (ACM)
SIG/IAC	Special Interest Group Information Analysis Centers (ASIS)
SIGIR	Special Interest Group on Information Retrieval (ACM)
SIG/LA	Special Interest Group Library Automation and Networks (ASIS)

SIGLASH	Special Interest Group on Language Analysis and Studies in the Humanities (ACM)
SIGMA	Science in General Management
SIGMAP	Special Interest Group on Mathematical Programming (ACM)
SIGME	Special Interest Group on Measurement and Evaluation (ACM)
SIGMICRO	Special Interest Group on Microprogramming (ASIS)
SIG/NPM	Special Interest Group on Non-Print Media (ASIS)
SIGNUM	Special Interest Group on Numerical Mathematics (ACM)
SIGOPS	Special Interest Group on Operating Systems (ACM)
SIGPLAN	Special Interest Group on Programming Languages (ACM)
SIGREAL	Special Interest Group on Real Time Processing (ACM)
SIG/RT	Special Interest Group Reprographic Technology (ASIS)
SIGSAM	Special Interest Group on Symbolic and Algebraic Manipulation (ACM)
SIG/SDI	Special Interest Group Selective Dissemination of Information (ASIS)
SIGSIM	Special Interest Group on Simulation (ACM)
SIGSOC	Special Interest Group on Social and Behavioral Science Computing (ACM)

SIGSPAC	Special Interest Group on Urban Data Systems, Planning, Architecture, and Civil Engineering (ACM)
SIG/TIS	Special Interest Group on Technology, Information, and Society (ASIS)
SIGUCC	Special Interest Group on University Computing Centers (ACM)
SIG/UOI	Special Interest Group on User On-line Interaction (ASIS)
SII	Standards Institute of Israel
SILLIAC	ILLIAC Computer at University of Sydney, Australia
SIM	Simulation
SIMBAD	Simulation as a Basis for Social Agent's Decisions
SIMCOM	Simulator Compiler
SIMCON	Console-based Simulation Language
SIMCON	Scientific Inventory Management and Control System
SIMON	Simulation Programming Language
SIMPAC	Simplified Programming for Acquisition and Control
SIMPAC	Simulation Programming Language
SIMPAL	Simplified Accounting Language (University of Wisconsin)
SIMPLE	Simple Intuitive Multipurpose Language
SIMPLE	Simulation Programming Language
SIMPLETRAN	Simple FORTRAN

SIMSCRIPT	Simulation Programming Language
SIMSCRIPT 1.5	SIMSCRIPT with modification
SIMSCRIPT II	SIMSCRIPT 1.5 with modifications
SIMULA	Simulation Language
SIN	Sine
SINH	Hyperbolic Sine
SIOP	Selector Input/Output Processors
SIOUX	Sequential and Iterative Operation Unit X Groups (block diagram language)
SIP	Simulated Input Processor
SIP	Societies for Information Processing (Denmark, Finland, Iceland, Norway and Sweden)
SIP	Symbolic Input Program
SIPE	TSS/360 Software Measurement Technique
SIPROS	Simultaneous Processing Operating System (CDC)
SIPS	Simulated Input Preparation System
SIR	Automatic Coding System
SIR	Selective Information Retrieval
SIR	Statistical Information Retrieval
SIR	Symbolic Input Routine
SIRS	Salary Information Retrieval System
SIS	Simulation Interface System
SIS	Society Information Systems
SITREP	Situation Report
SJ	*Simulation Journal*

SJAM	*SIAM Journal on Applied Mathematics*
SJCC	Spring Joint Computer Conference
SJNA	*SIAM Journal on Numerical Analysis*
SKETCHPAD	Man-Machine Graphical Communication System
SKP	Skip
SL	Source Language
SL	Storage Location
SL-1	Simulation Language One
SLA	Special Libraries Association
SLAC	Stanford Linear Accelerator Center
SLAMS	Simplified Language for Abstract Mathematical Structures
SLANG	Programming Language for Russian Computers
SLANG	User Oriented Programming Language
SLAP	Automatic Coding System
SLASH	Seiler Laboratory Algol Simulated Hybrid (Burroughs B-5500)
SLC	Simulated Linguistic Computer
SLD	Solid Logic Dense (IBM)
SLE	Society of Logistics Engineers
SLEUTH	Assembly Language (UNIVAC computers)
SLIP	Symmetric List Processor (List Processing Programming Language)
SLIS	Shared Laboratory Information System (IBM)

SLOPE	Slope Stability
SLP	Segmented Level Programming
SLP	Source Language Processor
SLT	Solid Logic Technique (IBM)
SLTF	Shortest-Latency-Time-First
SM	Shared Memory
SMA	Systems Management Association
SMALGOL	Small-computer Algorithmic Language
SMART	Programming Language
SMART	System Management and Review Technique
SMD	Scheduling Management Display
SME	Society of Manufacturing Engineers
SMIS	Society for Management Information Systems
SML	Symbolic Machine Language
SML	Symbolic Mathematical Laboratory
SMS	Standard Modular System of Packaging (IBM)
SN	Sign
S/N	Signal-to-Noise Ratio
SNACS	SHARE News on Automatic Coding Systems
SNAP	Simplified Numerical Automatic Programmer
SNAP	Text Processing Programming Language
SNOBOL	String-Oriented Symbolic Language

SNOOP	Information Retrieval Technique
SNUG	Scientific Users Group (NCR)
SO	Shop Order
SOAP I	Symbolic Optimum Assembly Programming One (IBM 650)
SOAP II	Symbolic Optimum Assembly Programming Two (IBM 650)
SOAP III	An Improved SOAP
SOC	Society
SOC	System Organization Compiler
SOCRATES	Scheduling of Classes Realized Automatically Through Effortless Systemization
SOCRATES	System for Organizing Content to Review and Teach Educational Subjects
SODA	Source Oriented Data Acquisition
SODAS	Structure Oriented Description and Simulation
SOFT	Simple Output Format Translator
SOL	Simulation Oriented Language
SOL	Systems Oriented Language
SOLID	Self-Organizing Large Information Dissemination System
SOLIS	Symbionics On-Line Information System
SOLVE	Compiler Language (Honeywell)
SOM	Start of Message
SOMADA	Self-Organizing Multiple-Access Discrete-Address

SONIC	Systemwide On-line Network for Informational Control (Continental Airlines)
SOP	Standard Operating Procedure
SOR	Start of Record
SOS	SHARE Operating System
SOS	Symbolic Operating System
SO/SI	Shift In and Shift Out
SOT	Syntax-Oriented Translator
SOTUS	Sequentially Operated Teletypewriter Universal Selector
SP	Single Purpose
SP	Special Purpose
SP	Standard Program
SP	Start Point
SP	Symbol Programmer
SP	System Processor
SP	Systems and Procedures
SPA	Southern Psychological Association
SPA	Southwestern Psychological Association
SPA	System Problem Area
SPA	Systems and Procedures Association
SPAC	Spatial Computer (Bell Labs)
SPACE	Sales Profitability and Contribution Evaluator
SPACE	Self-Programming Automatic Circuit Evaluator

SPACE	SPAR ALCOM COBOL Executive Program
SPADATS	Space Detection and Tracking System
SPADE	Spare Parts Analysis Documentation and Evaluation
SPANTRAN	Spanish FORTRAN
SPAR	Automatic Coding System
SPAR	Symbolic Program Assembly Routine
SPARTAN	System for Personnel: Automatic Records, Transactions, and Notices
SPASM	System Performance and Activity Software Monitor
SPASUR	Space Surveillance System
SPAT	Silicon Precision Alloy Transistor
SPC	Computer model series of General Automation Inc.
SPC	Single Prime Contractor
SPC	Stored Program Control
SPC	Stored Programmed Command
SPDP	Society of Professional Data Processors
SPEAKEASY	A communication network language
SPEC	Specification
SPEC	Stored Program Educational Computer
SPEDAC	Solid-state Parallel Expandable Differential Analyzer Computer
SPEDE	State System for Processing Educational Data Electronically (Florida)

SPEDTAC	Stored Program Educational Transistorized Automatic Computer
SPEED	Self-Programmed Electronic Equation Delineator
SPEEDCO	Automatic Coding System
SPEEDCODE	Automatic Programming System
SPEEDEX	Programming Language
SPERT	Schedule Performance Evaluation and Review Technique
SPES	Stored Program Element System (ITT)
SPG	Sort Program Generator
SPIB	Society for Programmed Instruction in Belgium
SPIE	Simulated Problem, Input Evaluation
SPIN	Sector Programming Leader
SPL	Spaceborne Programming Language
SPL	Space Programming Language
SPL	Student Programming Language
SPLINTER	Scientific PL/1 Interpreter
SPLIT	Sunstrand Processing Language Internally Translated
SPM	Sequential Processing Machines
SPM	Source Program Maintenance
SPM	Symbol Processing Machine
SPO-1	Debugging System (Strela Computer)
SPOOK	Supervisor Program Over Other Kinds
SPOOL	Spool System (IBM computer)
SPRINT	List Processing Language

SPRINT	Selective Printing
SPS	Samples Per Second
SPS	Symbolic Programming System
SPT	Symbolic Program Tape
SPT	Symbolic Program Translator
SPU	Sense Punch
SPUD	Statistical Package Utilizing Disk
SPUR	Automatic Coding System
SPURT	Symbolic Assembly Language (UNIVAC 490 series)
SPX	Simplex
SQ	Square
SQC	Statistical Quality Control
SQRT	Square Root
SR	Shift Register
SRS	Service Routine System
SRS	Student Response System
SS	Samples per Second
SS	Solid State
SS	Space Simulator
SS	Storage to Storage Instruction
SSEC	Selective Sequence Electronic Calculator
SSI	Swedish Society for Information Processing
SSIP	Swedish Society for Information Processing
SSP	Scientific Subroutine Package (IBM System/360 computer)

SSS	Scientific Subroutine System
SSS	Student Scheduling System
SSS	System Safety Society
SSSS	Stanford School Scheduling System
ST	Start
ST	Store
ST	System Test
STAMP	Systems Tape Addition and Maintenance Program
STAR	Automatic Coding System
STAR	Scientific and Technical Aerospace Reports
STAR	Self-Testing and Repairing Computer
STARFIRE	System To Accumulate and Retrieve Financial Information with Random Extraction
STARS	Satellite Telemetry Automatic Reduction System
START	Systematic Tabular Analysis of Requirements Technique
STATPAC	Statistics Package
STC	Standard Transmission Code
STD	Standard
STEP	Simple Transition to Economical Processing (UNIVAC)
STEP	Standard Tape Executive Package
STEP	Supervisory Tape Executive Program (NCR)
STET	Specialized Technique for Efficient Typesetting (Honeywell)

STI	Scientific and Technical Information
STM	System Master Tape
STMIS	System Test Manufacturing Information System (IBM)
STOR	Storage
STORM	Statistically Oriented Matrix Program
STP	Selective Tape Print
STP	System Test Procedure
STP	System Training Program
STPO	Science and Technology Policy Office
STR	Synchronous Transmitter Receiver
STRAP	STRETCH Assembly Program (IBM 7030 computer)
STRELIA	Russian Digital Computer
STRESS	Structural Engineering Systems Solver (M.I.T.)
STRETCH	IBM 7030 computer
STRIL	String Language
STRING	String Processing Systems
STROBES	Shared-Time Repair of Big Electronic Systems
STRUDL	Structural Design Language
STWP	Society of Technical Writers and Publishers
SU	Storage Unit
SUB	Subtract
SUMMIT	Supervisor of Multiprogramming, Multiprocessing, Interactive Timesharing (CDC computer)

SUNY	State University of New York
SUP	Basic Processing Supervisor (IBM 1800)
SUPERNOVA	Computer manufactured by DGC
SUPER SOAP	An Improved SOAP (Case Institute of Technology)
SURE	Symbolic Utility Revenue Environment (IBM)
SURF	Support of Users Records and Files
SURGE	Sorting Updating, Report Generating, Etc.
SWAC	Standards Western Automatic Computer (NBC)
SWAP	CDC Users Association
SWE	Society of Women Engineers
SW/FR	Slow-Write Fast-Read
SWIFT	Software Implemented Friden Translator
SY	Synchronized
SYDAS	System Data Acquisition System
SYMAN	Symbol Manipulation
SYMBAL	Symbolic Algebra
SYMBOL	Assembler (Xerox computers)
SYMPAC	Symbolic Program for Automatic Control (UNIVAC)
SYMPL	System Programming Language
SYN	Synchronous
SYNC	Synchronize
SYN SEM	Syntax and Semantics

SYS	System
SYSGEN	Systems Generation
SYSIN	System Input
SYSPOP	System Programmed Operator
SYSTEM/3	Family of IBM Computers
SYSTEM/360	Family of IBM Computers
SYSTEM/370	Family of IBM Computers
SYSTRAN	Systems Analysis Translator
SYSTST	System Test Program
SZ	Size

T

T	Temperature
T	Teracycle (one million megacycles per second)
T	Terminal
T	Time
T	Training
TA	Training Analyst
TAB	Tabular Language
TAB	Technical Abstract Bulletin
TABLE	Table Information
TABS	Terminal Access to Batch Service
TABSIM	Tabulator Simulator (Honeywell)
TABSOL	Tabular Systems Oriented Language
TAC	TRANSAC Assembler Compiler (Philco computer)
TAC	Transformer Analog Computer
TAC	Transistorized Automatic Control
TAC	Translator - Assembler - Compiler
TACPOL	Tactical Procedure Oriented Language
TACS	Tactical Air Control System
TACT	Technological Aids to Creative Thought
TACT	Transitor and Component Tester
TADPS	Tactical Army Data Processing System

TADS	Teletypewriter Automatic Dispatch System
TAI	Traditionally Administered Instruction
TALK	Take-A-Look (UNIVAC Debugging Language)
TAM	Theoretical Automatic Moron
TAMCO	Training Aid for MOBIDIC Console Operators
TAMS	Transactions of the American Mathematical Society
TAN	Tangent
TANH	Hyperbolic Tangent
TAP	Time-sharing Assembly Program
TAP	TRANSAC Assembly Program
TAPAC	Tape Automatic Positioning and Control
TAPE	Tape Automatic Preparation Equipment
TARAN	Tactical Attack Radar and Navigation
TARFU	Things Are Really Fouled Up
TARMOCS	The Army Operations Center System
TARS	Three Axes Reference System
TASC	Tabular Sequence Control
TASC	Terminal Area Sequence and Control
TASCON	Television Automatic Sequence Control
TAS-PAC	Total Analysis System for Planning, Accounting and Control
TASS	Tech Assembly System

TAT	Turn Around Time
TAWCS	Tactical Air Weapons Control System
TBL	Table
TC	Tactical Computer
TC	Terminal Computer
TC	Transfer Control
TC	Transmission Control
TCA	Tele-Communications Association
TCAI	Tutorial Computer-Assisted Instruction
TCC	Technical Computing Center
TCL	Table Creating Language
TCL	Tymshare Conversational Language
TCM	Terminal-to-Computer Multiplexer
TCPC	Tab Card Punch Control
TCU	Tape Control Unit
TCWG	Telecommunications Working Group
TD	Tabular Data
TD	Transmitter-Distributor
TD	Tunnel Diodes
TDG	Test Data Generator
TDMA	Time Division Multiple Access
TDMS	Time-Shared Data Management System
TDOS	Tape/Disk Operating System
TE	Test Equipment
T & E	Test and Evaluation
TEACH	Interpretive Programming Language (Honeywell)

TECH	Technology
TECO	Programming Language (DEC)
TEKHNOLOG-67	Programming Language for Russian Computers
TELCOMP	Interactive Programming Language
TELEFUNKEN	Allgemeine Electriniclatics-Gesellschaft (West German computer manufacturer)
TELE-PROCESSING	Data Communication Systems (IBM)
TELEX	Automatic Teletypewriter Exchange Service (Western Union)
TELSIM	Teletypewriter Simulation Language
TEMP	Temporary
TEMPO	Total Evaluation of Management and Production Output
TEX	Automatic Teleprinter Exchange Service (Western Union)
TEX	Telex
TF	Training Film
TFT	Thin Film Technology
TFT	Thin Film Transistor
TGS	Translator Generator System
THOMIS	Total Hospital Operating and Medical Information System
THOPS	Tape Handling Operational System
THOR	Tape Handling Option Routines
THREE-D	Perspective Drawing Software System (CALCOMP)
TI	Tape Inverter
TIC	FORTRAN Editing Program

TIC	Tape Intersystem Connection
TIC	Target Intercept Computer (UNIVAC)
TICS	Teacher Interactive Computer System
TIES	Transmission and Information Exchange System
TIMM	Thermionic Integrated Micro Modules
TIMS	The Information Management System
TIMS	The Institute of Management Science
TINT	On-line Teletype JOVIAL Interpreter
TIP	Data Management System
TIP	Technical Information Processing
TIP	Total Information Processing
TIPI	Tactical Information Processing and Interpretation
TIPL	Teach Information Processing Language
TIPTOP	Tape Input - Tape Output
TIS	Total Information System
TIU	Tape Identification Unit
TKC	Takachiho Koheki Co. (Japanese computer manufacturer)
TL	Tape Library
TL	Target Language
TLM	Telemetry
TLP	Total Language Processor
TLU	Table Look Up
TM	Tape Mark

TMCC	Time-Multiplexed Communication Channel
TMG	Syntax-directed Compiling Language
TMP	Temperature
TMR	Triple Modular Redundancy
TMS	Time-shared Monitor System (IBM)
TO	Trade Off
TOC	Table of Contents
TOCS	Technological Aids to Creative Thought
TOD	Time Of Day
TOL	Test Oriented Language
TOL	Transactions On Line
TOOL	Processor Construction Language
TOPP	Terminal Operated Production Program (IBM)
TOPS	Teletype Optical Projection System
TOPS	Testing and Operating System
TOPS	Total Operations Processing System
TOS	Tape Operating System
TOS	Terminal-Oriented Software
TOS	Terminal-Oriented System
TOSBAC	Toshiba Scientific and Business Automatic Computer
TOSHIBA	Tokyo Shibaura Electric Co. (Japanese computer manufacturer)
TOTALTRAN	Autocoder to IBM System/360 Assembly Language Translator

TOTE	Relay Computer for Parimutuel Computations at Race Track
TP	Tape
TP	Technical Publication
TP	Tele-Processing
TP	Test Procedure
TPM	Tape Preventive Maintenance
TPR	Teleprinter
TPU	Tape Preparation Unit
TR	Tape Recorder
TRAC	Text Reckoning And Compiling (a keyboard language)
TRACE	Tape-controlled Recording Automatic Checkout System
TRACE	Time-shared Routines for Analysis, Classification and Evaluation
TRACE	Transportable Automated Control Environment
TRADIC	Transistor Digital Computer
TRAIN	Tele-Rail Automated Information Network
TRAMP	Time-shared Relational Associative Memory Program
TRANDIR	Translation Director (syntax-directed compiling language)
TRANGEN	Compiler Writing System
TRANQUIL	Programming Language (based on ALGOL)
TRANSAC	Transistorized Automatic Computer (Philco Corp.)

TRANSCODE	Automatic Coding System (FERUT—University of Toronto)
TRAWL	Tape Read And Write Library
TRC	Tape Record Coordinator
TREET	List Processing Language (similar to LISP)
TRICE	Transistorized Real Time Incremental Computer
TRIG	Trigonometry
TRIM	Critical Path Program
TRIM	Test Rules for Inventory Management
TRN	Transfer
TROS	Tape Resident Operating System
TRP	Digital Computer (mfg. by the German firm Telefunken)
TRTL	Transistor-Resistor Transistor Logic
TRUMP	Teller-Register Unit Monitoring Program
TS	Temporary Storage
TS	Time-Sharing
TS	Top Secret
TSDM	Time-Shared Data Management System
TSDOS	Time-Shared Disk Operating System
TSF	Thin Solid Films
TSIMOD	Programming Language for Russian Computers
TSM	Time-shared Monitor System
TSO	Time Sharing Option

TSOS	Time-Sharing Operating System
TSPS	Time-Sharing Programming System
TSS	Time-Sharing System
TSS/8	Time-Sharing System (PDP-8 computer)
TSX	Time-Sharing Executive (IBM 1800)
TT	Teletypewriter
TTC	Tape to Card
TTL	Teletype Telling
TTL	Transistor-Transistor Logic
TTP	Tape to Print
TTY	Teletype Unit
TTY	Teletypewriter
TU	Tape Unit
TUCC	Triangle Universities Computation Center (North Carolina)
TUG	TRANSAC Users Group (Philco 2000)
TV	Television
TWX	Teletypewriter Exchange Service
TX	Transmit
TYDAC	Typical Digital Automatic Computer

U

U	Unit
U	Utility
UADPS	Uniform Automatic Data Processing System
UAIDE	Users of Automatic Information Display Equipment
UAIMS	United Aircraft Information Management System
UBC	Universal Buffer Controller
UC	Upper Case
UCS	Universal Character Set
UCS	Universal Classification System
UCW	Unit Control Word
UDC	Universal Decimal Classification
UDEC	Unitized Digital Electronic Calculator (Burroughs Corp.)
UDOFTT	Universal Digital Operational Flight Trainer Tool (Sylvania)
UDP	United Data Processing
UGLIAC	United Gas Laboratory Internally-Programmed Automatic Computer
UHF	Ultrahigh Frequency
UIL	Univac Interactive Language
UKCIS	United Kingdom Chemical Information Service
UL-1	User Language 1 (programming language for document and library applications)

ULC	Universal Logic Circuit
ULTRA-X	Universal Language for Typegraphic Reproduction Applications
UM-1	Russian Computer
UMAC	University of Miami Algebraic Compiler
UMAP	University of Michigan Assembly Program
UMASS	Unlimited Machine Access from Scattered Sites (Univ. of Massachusetts)
UMC	Polish Digital Computer
UMSLN	Russian Computer
UNAMAC	Universal Computer Oriented Compilation Equipment
UNCOL	Universal Computer Oriented Language
UNICODE	UNIVAC Automatic Coding System (A language similar to MATH-MATIC)
UNICOMP	Universal Compiler for Process Control
UNICON	Unidensity Coherent Light Recording
UNIMIS	Unified Management Information System
UNIPLOT	Plotting Routine (UNIVAC computer)
UNIPOL	Universal Procedures-Oriented Language
UNISAP	UNIVAC Share Assembly Program
UNITRAC	Universal Trajector Compiler
UNIV	University

UNIVAC	Division of Sperry Rand Corporation
UNIVAC	Universal Automatic Computer
UPADI	Pan-American Federation of Engineering Societies
UPDATE	Unlimited Potential Data through Automation Technology in Education (Iowa State University)
UPL	Universal Programming Language
UPLIFTS	University of Pittsburgh Linear File Tandem System
UPOS	Utility Program Operating System
UR	Unit Record
URAL	Russian Digital Computer
US	Microsecond; one-millionth of a second
USA SC	USA Standards Committee
USASCII	U.S.A. Standard Code for Information Interchange
USASCSOCR	USA Standard Character Set for Optical Character Recognition
USASI	United States of America Standards Institute (now ANSI)
USE	UNIVAC Scientific Exchange
U SEC	Microsecond; one-millionth of a second
USEC	United System of Electronic Computers
USOE	U.S. Office of Education
UT	Up Time
UT	Utility

UTMOST	UNIVAC Machine Oriented Language (UNIVAC III)
UTS	Unified Transfer System
UTS	Universal Time-Sharing Monitor (Xerox Sigma Series)
UTTC	Universal Tape to-Tape Converter
UUA	UNIVAC Univac Users Association
UUT	Unit Under Test
UWBASIC	University of Washington BASIC
UWBIC	University of Washington BASIC Interpretive Compiler

V

V	Verbal
V	Video
V	Voice
V	Volt
V	Voltage
VAB	Voice Answer Back
VADE	Versatile Auto Data Exchange
VAMP	Vector Arithmetic Multi-Processor
VARS	Vertical Azimuth Reference System
VASCAR	Visual Average Speed Computer and Recorder
VAT	Virtual Address Translator
VATE	Versatile Automatic Test Equipment
VCC	Visual Communications Congress
VCS	Victorian Computer Society
V/D	Voice/Data
VDE	Verband Deitscher Elektrotechniker (Association of German Electrical Engineers)
VDM	Varian Data Machines
VDP	Vertical Data Processing
VEPIS	Vocational Education Program Information System
VER	Verification
VF	Voice Frequency

VFU	Vertical Format Unit
VHF	Very High Frequency
VHM	Virtual Hardware Monitor
VIC	Variable Instruction Computer
VIDAC	Visual Information Display and Control
VIDAT	Visual Data Acquisition
VIDEOSCAN	Optical Character Reader
VIM	CDC 6000 Series Users Organization
VINITE AL	All-Union Institute of Scientific and Technical Information (U.S.S.R.)
VIP	Variable Information Processing
VIP	Visual Information Projection (Honeywell)
VIPP	Variable Information Processing Package
VLF	Variable Length Field
VLF	Very Low Frequency
VM	Virtual Machine
VM	Virtual Memory
VMM	Virtual Machine Monitor
VMTSS	Virtual Machine Time-Sharing System
VNIIEM	Russian Computer Prefix
VODACOM	Voice Data Communications
VOL	Volume
VRC	Vertical Redundancy Check
VRC	Visual Record Computer

VS	Variable Speed
VS	Virtual Storage
VSAM	Virtual Storage Access Method
VT	Vacuum Tube
VT	Video Tape
VTCS	Vehicular Traffic Control System (IBM 1800)
VTOC	Volume Table of Contents
VTR	Video Tape Recorder
VU	Voice Unit
VWL	Variable Word Length

W

W	Watts
WADS	Wide Area Data Service
WALNUT	Information Retrieval System (IBM)
WAP	Work Assignment Procedure
WATFOR	FORTRAN IV Compiler (University of Waterloo)
WATS	Wide Area Telephone Service
WB	Wide Band
WCS	Writable Control Store
WD	Word
WDPC	Western Data Processing Center (University of California at Los Angeles)
WEDAC	Westinghouse Digital Airborne Computer
WEIZAC	Israel's First Computer (Weizmann Institute of Science in Rehovot)
WEMA	Western Electronic Manufacturers Association
WESCOM	Weapons System Cost Model
WESCON	Western Electronic Show and Convention
WETAC	Westinghouse Electronic Tubeless Analog Computer
WHIRLWIND	Digital Computer (M.I.T.)
WHIZ	Programming Language
WIP	Work In Progress

WISAL	Wisconsin Accounting Language
WISC	Wisconsin Integrally Synchronized Computer (University of Wisconsin)
WIZ	Algebraic and Tabular Language
WIZOR	Compiler Language
WJCC	Western Joint Computer Conference
W/M	Words per Minute
WNRC	Washington National Records Center
WO	Work Order
WOM	Write Optional Memory
WPM	Words Per Minute
WPS	Words Per Second
WR	Write
WRURS	Western Reserve University Retrieval System
W/S	Words per Second
WTS	Word Terminal Synchronous
WU	Western Union
WWI	Whirlwind I
WWII	Whirlwind II

X

X	Experimental
XACT	X Automatic Code Translation
XEROX	Computer division of Xerox Corp.
XFER	Transfer
XMIT	Transmit
XMITS	Transmits
XMT	Transmit
XMTG	Transmitting
XMTL	Transmittal
XMTR	Transmitter
X-OFF	Transmitter Off
X-ON	Transmitter On
XOS	XEROX Operating System
XPOP	Meta-Language Programming System Experimental Languages (IBM)
XS-3	Excess-3 Code
XTRAN	Time-Sharing Programming Language

Y

Y-PUNCH	Top Row Card Punch
YR	Year

Z

Z	Zero Suppression Symbol
ZEBRA	Programming Language (Electrologica XI computer)
ZENIT-3	Russian Computer
ZMMD	Zurich, Mainz, Munich, Darmstadt (A joint university effort on ALGOL processors)
ZN	Zone
ZOOM	Macroassembler (GE-235 computer)
ZRA	Digital Computer (German)
ZUSE	Zuse K.G. (West German computer manufacturer)